"Authentic, appropriate and timely, *When Teachers Stay* validates educator voices while speaking directly to school leaders. Through the presentation of anecdotal evidence and research, Hughes explains what can be done to address teacher retention within school settings."

Kanoe Bunney, PhD, *Professor of Education, Linn Benton Community College*

"*When Teachers Stay: Cultivating Resilient Teaching Communities* is a wonderful contribution at a most important time. This book is written at a time when questions of staying power and resilience are needed to meet the challenges of this ambiguous and uncertain time. Michelle has the heart of an artist combined with the practicality of an exceptional school leader. She provides an excellent critical analysis of the meaning of resilience as she integrates the work of others with her research in the field. She shows how to sustain the values of a school culture through agile and thoughtful processes that develop a community of educators built for resilience."

Bena Kallick, *Co-Director, The Institute for Habits of Mind*

"As life in our schools becomes more uncertain by the day, this book promotes a return to the joy we felt when we entered the education profession. Through compelling conversations with a wide array of educators, soulful reflections and invitations for the reader to reflect and act, *When Teachers Stay* elegantly unpacks a series of resilience intentions which include curiosity, collegiality, celebration and support. Hughes has provided school leaders a book for our times."

David Levine, *Founder/Director, Teaching Empathy Institute*

When Teachers Stay

Why do some schools have high levels of teacher turnover, but others don't? This powerful book explores the question of what makes a resilient teaching community in which teachers want to stay and thrive. Author Michelle Hughes embarks on a journey, including school visits and conversations with teachers and school leaders, to uncover the cohesiveness, continuity, community, and deep sense of belonging for adults and kids that occurs in some schools.

In Part 1, Hughes describes the conditions that foster such a community, including trust, belonging, collaboration, and a culture of ongoing growth and shared decision-making. Part 2 explores the essential role leaders play in providing those conditions. In Part 3, you'll learn the roles teachers play in building collaboration, autonomy and community, conflict, and shared mission or vision. Part 4 focuses on the impacts of resilient teaching communities on the child's educational journey from pre-kindergarten to twelfth grade. It also explores the obstacles faced by the leaders and teachers who are invested in cultivating their own resilient teaching community. And finally, at the end of each chapter, you'll have opportunities for reflection and action so you can bring the ideas back to your own school.

From rural Indiana to New York City, teachers have shared the same conditions that matter most to their feeling of community and longevity in their roles. Find out how your school can be a powerful place of belonging too.

Michelle Hughes, MEd, is an educator with more than thirty years of experience in teaching and leading in both public and independent schools. As a public school teacher, Michelle co-developed an integrated team approach to inclusion, which informed her work as a school leader. As an independent school leader, she began writing on topics in education and chronicling the daily life of school. As a founder and director of Learning Arts Consulting and Coaching, she now works with schools in a variety of areas including Habits of Mind. Certified by the Institute for the Habits of Mind, Michelle wrote the *Habits of Mind Playbook*, a guide for integrating habits of mind into classroom curricula and culture.

Also Available from Routledge Eye On Education

www.routledge.com/K-12

Invest in Your Best: 9 Strategies to Grow, Support, and Celebrate Your Most Valuable Teachers
Todd Whitaker, Connie Hamilton, TJ Vari, Joseph Jones

How to Get All Teachers to Become Like the Best Teachers
Todd Whitaker

The Resilient School Leader: 20 Ways to Manage Stress and Build Resilience
Bryan Harris and Janet Gilbert

Embracing Adult SEL: An Educator's Guide to Personal Social Emotional Learning
Wendy Turner

Finding Your Leadership Edge: Balancing Assertiveness and Compassion in Schools
Brad Johnson and Jeremy Johnson

What Great Principals Do Differently, Third Edition: Twenty Things That Matter Most
Todd Whitaker

Active Literacy Across the Curriculum, Second Edition: Connecting Print Literacy with Digital, Media, and Global Competence, K-12
Heidi Hayes Jacobs

When Teachers Stay
Cultivating Resilient Teaching Communities

Michelle Hughes

NEW YORK AND LONDON

Designed cover image: Getty Images

First published 2026
by Routledge
605 Third Avenue, New York, NY 10158

and by Routledge
4 Park Square, Milton Park, Abingdon, Oxon, OX14 4RN

Routledge is an imprint of the Taylor & Francis Group, an informa business

© 2026 Michelle Hughes

The right of Michelle Hughes to be identified as author of this work has been asserted in accordance with sections 77 and 78 of the Copyright, Designs and Patents Act 1988.

All rights reserved. No part of this book may be reprinted or reproduced or utilised in any form or by any electronic, mechanical, or other means, now known or hereafter invented, including photocopying and recording, or in any information storage or retrieval system, without permission in writing from the publishers.

Trademark notice: Product or corporate names may be trademarks or registered trademarks, and are used only for identification and explanation without intent to infringe.

ISBN: 978-1-041-08184-5 (hbk)
ISBN: 978-1-041-08183-8 (pbk)
ISBN: 978-1-003-64414-9 (ebk)

DOI: 10.4324/9781003644149

Typeset in Palatino
by codeMantra

To my parents, Esther and Herb Rosenfeld. Their passion for their work as educators, their courage in transforming schooling for thousands of kids in New York City, and the inspiration they provided for their own children to do work of meaning were my guiding light in writing this book.

Contents

Foreword: Heidi Hayes Jacobs xi

PART 1
What Is a Resilient Teaching Community? 1

  1 The Story of When Teachers Stay 3

  2 Defining a Resilient Teaching Community 9

PART 2
The Visible and Supportive Leader: Actively Cultivating Resilient Teaching Communities 17

  3 Visible Leaders Growing and Sustaining Resilient Teaching Communities 19

  4 Build Trust 28

  5 Forge a Community of Belonging 37

  6 Provide Opportunities for Ongoing Professional Growth 42

  7 Engage in Shared Decision-Making 55

PART 3
The Working Community 65

  8 Foster a Collaborative Environment 67

  9 Focus on Mission and Vision 81

PART 4
Obstacles, Impacts, and Reflections 95

10 Obstacles to Resilient Teaching Communities 97

11 Impacts of Resilient Teaching Communities 107

Final Thoughts 119
Acknowledgments 121
Sources 127

Foreword

by Heidi Hayes Jacobs

Resilience is explored, defined, documented, exalted, and imagined in an exceptionally wide array of learning settings in Michelle Hughes' *When Teachers Stay: Cultivating Resilient Teaching Communities.* When considering the etymology of any word, its very roots, by nature, get to its actual intent. The origin of *resilience* is from the Latin *resilientem* "inclined to leap or spring back," present participle of *resilire* "to jump back." It is a positive force, to come back and to rebound, yet there is something underneath that speaks to the unusual power of resilience. To rebound or spring back, the object or person or community in question must have gone through a difficult time, a challenge. They are, in fact, bouncing back from a difficult time. It is here that Hughes has found some astonishing truths that can serve all educators, providing stamina and even hope.

Deepening our understanding of the term in order to act and make a difference in the lives of both students and professionals is central to Michelle Hughes' book. In documenting the ways that resilience has been fostered and nurtured in learning communities, she shows how even under the most difficult circumstances when resilience is evident or even the seeds of resilience, not only do organizations survive, they bounce back having learned from the experience and can actually surge forward into a range of new possibilities. In short, resilience is more than surviving challenges; it is thriving over future iterations of a community.

In order to encourage constructive action, Hughes has shaped an operational definition of collective resilience that can be observed, analyzed, adjusted, and ultimately developed in a community. Central to her contention are Seven Essential Attributes of Resilience that must be observed and nurtured with keen deliberation by a community to sustain its power. I have summarized these seven actionable attributes as:

1. Leadership that sets reliance as a priority for all members of the community while providing the resources to undergird its cultivation.
2. Trust built and based upon consensually developed communication lanes and approaches to collaborative work.
3. A sense of belonging perceived by each and every teacher that they are seen and accepted.
4. Professional development on specific approaches to develop resilience that is ongoing and supported.
5. Shared decision-making in the community is central to key issues impacting the school and its learners.
6. Collaboration balancing autonomy and community throughout the system is evident on a daily basis.
7. Shared vision and mission is consistently and visibly led by administrators and by teachers on both a systems and classroom level.

Hughes has organized the chapters in this book around these seven attributes, which makes for easy reference. She employs powerful and varied case studies to support her attributes from a range of settings, both public and independent schools stretching from California to Indiana to New York to Pennsylvania to Maine. Her interviews with educators are rich with authentic and insightful reflections. What emerges is a clear picture of what happens when an educational community deepens and deliberately cultivates resilience, that is, each member of that community benefits and their learners soar with possibilities. Reading the honest commentary and specific observations of the educators featured in this book, it is obvious that Hughes has earned their trust and respect. Throughout this book, there were particular standout experiences that were quite literally boxed out to call attention to key findings that Hughes has observed whether it's Collaborative and Supportive leadership in East Greenbush Central School District, East Greenbush, New York or Resilient Teaching Communities in Two International Habits of Mind Learning Communities of Excellence in California.

Implementing her ideas is the fundamental point of this book, and Hughes gives the reader coaching on pitfalls and obstacles in the last sections of this book. Whether dealing with motivating all members of a community to gain attention to the resilience issue or wrestling with curriculum challenges that have turned political, she does not back away. Rather, she shares strategies and approaches based on her study and work with schools that are realistic.

In addition, there are practical addenda to each chapter, entitled: *Reflect. Act.* The reader will find a wealth of practical tools, resources, and strategies to use when working with faculty members or community groups on implementing the ideas she has developed. These tools include charts, graphs, and response sheets on how to gauge attitudes and perceptions in a community regarding belonging, values, and actions that might support the seven attributes Hughes has outlined.

Michelle Hughes has our backs. Through her methodical and inspired study over years of field work, she has elevated and clarified what community resilience means, how necessary it is for educators, and what actions we can take to create communities where all members belong and can contribute to our collective futures.

Part 1
What Is a Resilient Teaching Community?

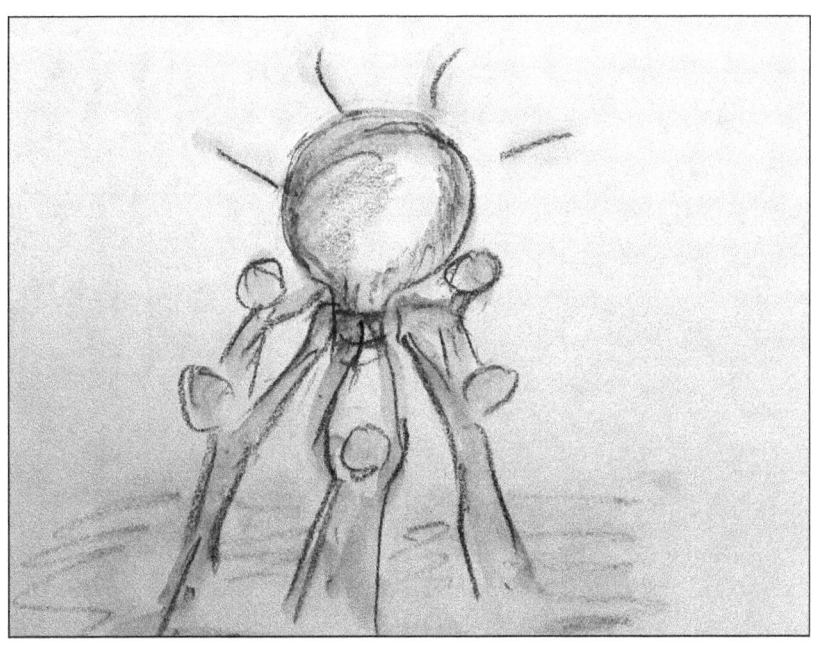

Illustration. What is a resilient teaching community. Michelle Hughes.

1
The Story of When Teachers Stay

As the COVID-19 pandemic waned in 2022, data began surfacing in journals and news reports about the extraordinary number of teachers leaving the profession. In fact, 2021–22 would prove to have the highest teacher attrition rate in a ten-year time frame (Nguyen 2022). Given that a significant number of states do not report this data, a conservative estimate is that over 300,000 teaching positions nationally are vacant or filled by under-qualified individuals (Franco and Kemper Patrick 2023). As a veteran and devoted observer of the education world, I was both alarmed to hear this and curious about its implications.

While I understood the factors that were driving teachers from the field—post-COVID burnout, school violence, mandates, and pay, to name a few—I was most curious about the schools that were not experiencing this level of upheaval. This inspired the question: *What are the conditions that foster environments where teachers are committed to stay?* Further, this question prompted an idea, a term for what I'd been formulating over more than thirty years of working in and visiting schools: *resilient teaching community*. This term captured the cohesiveness, continuity, community, and deep sense of belonging for adults and kids that I have witnessed in some schools.

Through my writing and ruminations on this idea, I decided to test and define it. Thus, I embarked on a journey that included school visits, conversations with teachers and school leaders, and explorations of literature within and beyond the educational domain—and found that *resilient teaching community* is a novel term encompassing long-understood but infrequently practiced community-building approaches. The writing that emerged from this process is *When Teachers Stay: Cultivating Resilient Teaching Communities*.

There is not an abundance of research on *resilient teaching communities* per se; however, the conditions that foster and the attributes that define resilient teaching communities have been studied within and beyond the world of education literature.

The Research Process

When Teachers Stay: Cultivating Resilient Teaching Communities asks and explores:

- ♦ What is a resilient teaching community?
- ♦ What are the conditions that foster these communities of teachers?
- ♦ What are these communities' attributes?
- ♦ What are the impacts of and obstacles to resilient teaching communities?

To answer these questions, I adopted bifurcated research pathways. One path led to primary research such as polls, interviews, on-site school visits, and correspondence. The other pathway is conventional research meant to place the ideas, experiences, and feelings of the participants in a larger context. Through examining and analyzing literature and studies on the efficacy of collaboration, professional learning, autonomy, and community, as well as the importance of belonging in one's school or workplace, I was able to establish the impacts that these conditions have on students, teaching and learning, and the larger community.

There are two categories of participants in this study: *participating schools* and *voices*. The schools I identified for participation were known for having high functioning teaching communities, for being great places to work, and/or demonstrating strong commitments to mission by faculty. The initial schools I approached were located in New York State and were varied in demographics, age ranges served, and geography. The East Greenbush Central School District, a public school district in New York's Capital Region, approximately 150 miles north of New York City, won a local press award for "Top Workplaces" for three years. There, I interviewed the superintendent and a collection of teachers. I visited with the school leaders and staff of Poughkeepsie Day School, an independent K–12 school that had closed due to financial hardship and is being revived through the generosity of a group of committed parents and the sweat equity of faculty and staff. I spent time at the Center School, a public middle school in Manhattan, part of the small schools of choice movement, with a long reputation of being a collaborative and empowering place to teach and learn.

As I broadened the geographic reach of the primary research, I reached out to Crystal Thorpe, the principal of Fishers Junior High School in Fishers, Indiana. Thorpe writes about the kind of leadership that leads to resilient teaching communities, and our correspondence led me to spend a day in her school, speaking with teachers and staff. I expanded the circle of participation to the leaders of the World of Learning Institute in Pennsylvania, a collaborative that provides online learning to districts that are short on instructors in second language and mathematics.

As I expanded my reach to individual voices, I connected with the principal of Duzine Elementary School in New Paltz, New York, Ross Hogan, a former student of mine and a relatively new principal. During a Habits of Mind conference in Vista, California, I interviewed school leaders and teachers from Habits of Mind-certified schools in Vista and Montecito, California, to get a sense of how a schoolwide commitment to a framework such as Habits of Mind helps build teaching communities. In addition, the voices of individual teachers and leaders with experience teaching and leading in resilient teaching communities—or in the process of cultivating one—are heard throughout the book. These conversations breathe life into the book and form the core around which the research is focused, driven by the content of the interviews, placing what teachers and school leaders say in a historical context, and connecting their assertions to evidence.

Who Should Read *When Teachers Stay: Cultivating Resilient Teaching Communities?*

When Teachers Stay is most of all a project borne from love for the educational process and the teachers and students engaged in it. Over some thirty years, I came up through the ranks of teaching to lead teams, then schools. My leadership perspective is, at the heart, one of a teacher. Interestingly, I found over the course of interviews for the book that teachers shared their own experiences of working in resilient teaching communities with the leadership of their schools in mind. Each and every school leader and teacher I interviewed pointed to the visible and supportive leadership as the primary condition for fostering and sustaining resilient teaching communities. This is supported by the research. Thus, this book is at its heart written for school leaders, for leaders play an indispensable role in cultivating resilient teaching communities. In reading, *When Teachers Stay*, school leaders will learn from other school leaders the rationale and building blocks for cultivating a resilient teaching community, and see that these communities thrive with the continuity and longevity of their leadership and the building of collective wisdom. School leaders will hear the voices of teachers sharing just how critical it is to feel the trust of their leaders. Leaders will understand how important it is for teachers to feel they are *seen* and their teaching practices are understood. At the end of each chapter is an opportunity for you to bring this into your work with your teaching community. Each of your schools is different, and your time is precious, so the activities guide you efficiently and succinctly to Reflect on your particular faculty, school, strengths and limitations, and then Act based on what you have identified as the possibilities.

While this book is aimed at leadership, it can offer insights to additional cohorts of stakeholders. In reading *When Teachers Stay*, teachers might find resonance and affirmation in how their peers describe their lived experiences in resilient teaching communities and find ways to open up channels for building community resilience in their own schools. School board members and trustees will see the importance of the cohesiveness of their leaders, faculty, and staff as a strength to be protected. Graduate leadership programs and leadership consultants may be inspired to embed the building blocks of resilient teaching communities into the education and training of school leaders. Because teachers so clearly benefit from the energy and work put into cultivating resilient teaching communities, teachers' unions might rethink how they work with districts to support such important work. A collaborative relationship between union locals and their schools can go a long way to ensuring a collaborative environment as a whole.

When Teachers Stay is not a treatise on nurturing the resilience of *individual* teachers. Much has been written and implemented in this arena. I also do not venture into the reasons for the high attrition rate in the teaching profession. There are many excellent resources that explore the complexity of reasons teachers leave. This book focuses on the question, what are the conditions that make teachers stay?

Organization of the Book

The chapters in *When Teachers Stay: Cultivating Resilient Teaching Communities* are entitled by the actions leaders can take to set the conditions for resilient teaching communities to flourish. They are organized into four parts:

Part 1: What is a Resilient Teaching Community explores the meaning of the term *resilient teaching community* and some of the experiences of educators working in resilient teaching communities. It offers answers to the questions: What are the principles, processes, and procedures a school's leader and faculty develop to cultivate and maintain a resilient teaching community? What are the conditions that foster resilient teaching communities?

Part 2: The Visible and Supportive Leader is dedicated to exploring the actions leaders will take to nurture resilience in their teaching community. These actions mirror the attributes teachers identified as hallmarks of resilient teaching communities.

- Visible and supportive leadership: Leading through well-understood systems of collaboration, support and responsibilities, and a commitment to visibility.
- Build trust through coming to know teachers and their work well.
- Know the professionals in the classrooms well, creating a sense of belonging and being known among them.
- Provide opportunities for ongoing professional growth through individual and group learning in school-based and external professional development.
- Share decision-making in well-understood facets of teaching and learning and school operations.

Part 3: The Working Community examines how the leaders establish resilient teaching communities as they:

- Foster a collaborative environment between and among faculty and school leadership, while balancing autonomy and community.
- Focus on Shared Vision and Mission in teaching and learning, decision-making, and ongoing professional development.

Part 4: Obstacles and Impacts focuses on the impacts of resilient teaching communities on the child's educational journey from pre-kindergarten to twelfth grade. Part 4 also explores the obstacles to the cultivation of resilient teaching communities, and what leaders and teachers who are invested in cultivating their own resilient teaching community face. We also visit two schools that have undergone leadership changes, to learn more about resilience in action.

The *Reflect. Act.* component of this book offers leaders a process at the end of each chapter for reflecting, information gathering, and cultivating trust, belonging, collaboration, shared decision-making, and ongoing growth. Let us now begin the journey by defining what we mean by resilient teaching communities. How do they benefit teaching and learning and nurture schoolwide well-being?

2

Defining a Resilient Teaching Community

The cultivation of resilient teaching communities requires rethinking and reprioritizing the roles and responsibilities of school leaders and teachers. School leaders will approach this undertaking differently based on mission, size, resources, demographics, and the particular history and obstacles they face. But the constants I found through these many conversations are seven **conditions** that leaders foster in order to cultivate resilient teaching communities. These conditions become the **attributes** of the resilient teaching community, as seen by teachers (Figure 2.1).

Leaders who support and prioritize the process of collaboration so valued by teachers, who are visibly spending time in classrooms and with community members, are able to identify the resources needed for teachers to flourish.

Trust is seen as a precondition for all the other attributes to grow. Participants articulated further that **trust** is built and preserved through agreed-upon ways of communicating, working, and learning together. Striving toward common goals leads to leader-teacher synchronicity.

When teachers **feel seen** and **accepted as professionals**, teachers are able to fully engage as well as to accept others in their teaching community.

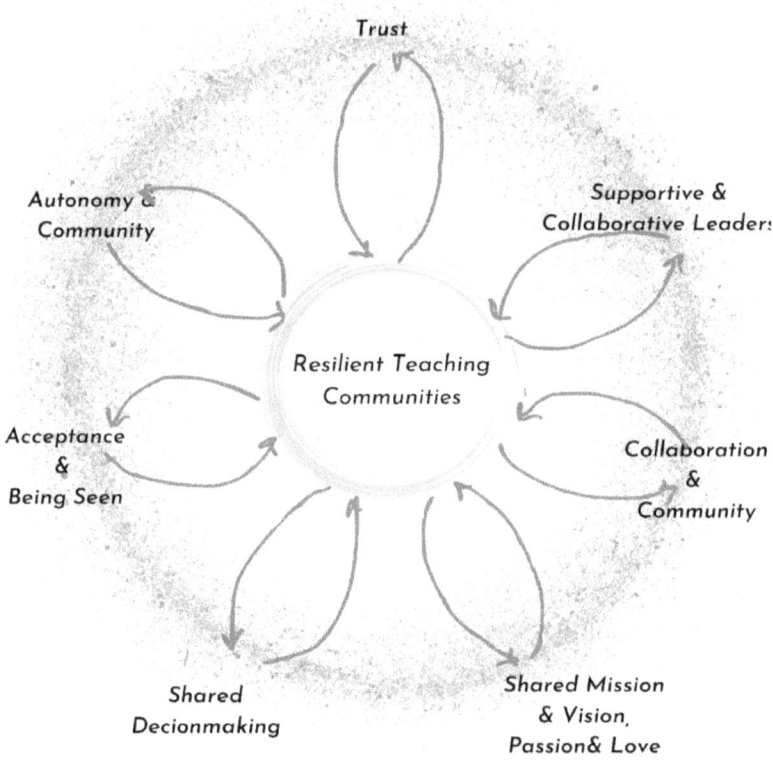

FIGURE 2.1 The Conditions and Attributes of a Resilient Teaching Community Artist, Michelle Hughes.

Opportunities for **ongoing professional growth** are highly valued along with time and follow-up to integrate the learning into daily teaching and learning, or systems practices.

Shared decision-making is a hallmark of these schools' operations in which teachers feel ownership of their schools. This is where the community does its hard work of problem-solving and facing difficulty—whether with a child or a pandemic—and builds its resilience.

Collaboration among and between teaching and administrative cohorts and the **balancing between autonomy and community** are woven into planning, initiatives, and day-to-day systems in the school.

A **shared mission and vision** is supported by or established through collaborative processes, advanced by the school leader, and achieved through the commitments and work of the whole.

The Process

Way back at the beginning, when I was seeking a definition of resilient teaching communities I floated out two LinkedIn surveys. In the first, I ran a poll to determine which of four *conditions* people considered most significant in fostering a resilient teaching community. The participants could choose more than one, and the sixteen responses broke out as follows:

- A supportive and collaborative administration: 72%
- Adequate resources: 14%
- A common purpose or philosophy: 14%
- Faculty camaraderie: 14%

As one participant wrote in response to this first poll, "The bottom three (conditions) are all necessary, and none sufficient unto themselves without the first."

I also received comments such as: "All four," and "I can't choose." The limitations of the poll's structure, which allowed for one choice rather than a ranking, make the verbal responses important. And yet, the significance of a supportive and collaborative administrator rang out as a critical condition to fostering resilience in teaching communities.

In the second poll, participants were asked, "What are the *attributes* of a resilient teaching community?" The answers were as follows:

- Adaptable innovative faculty, 40%
- Diverse inclusive culture, 20%
- Site-based decision-making, 40%
- High teacher retention 0%

The results for this poll were sparse; however, what was notable was participants gave high teacher retention as an attribute of a resilient teaching community, 0%. It was illuminating that resiliency and retention were not seen as synonymous by the people who answered the poll or followed up with comments. In an effort to retain teachers, school leadership and consultants focused on building individual teachers' resilience, particularly during the pandemic. But participating teachers themselves did not necessarily equate resilience with retention. After all, leaving education, which might be among the hardest decisions an educator ever makes, may be a reflection of healthy personal resilience.

Taken by the negative correlation between resilient teaching communities and retention response, I incorporated that question into my interviews with participants. My first interviewee was a pioneering educator, director of Central Park East II, in East Harlem, New York City, and Bank Street College of Education's Leadership Institute, Esther Rosenfeld, who also happens to be my mother. She resolutely stated, "Resilience is the steely resolve to keep at the work. It's the making more with less, and the independence to solve problems instead of expecting others (like the system) to do it. Retention is simply staying."

As Lauren DeGeorgia, world language teacher and middle school dean at the Albany Academies, shared, "Resilience is a reflection of how people are working together day to day, but it is also reducing turnover because you have people who know how to work together and have known students and their families." Many participants believe there is a relationship between a resilient teaching community and teacher retention, but a resilient teaching community is not defined solely by retention.

Resilience, in pure terms, is the ability to bounce back from challenges. In conversation after conversation, educators told me they saw the resilience in their schools as a collective and generative response to challenge. Elaine Chu, a longtime teacher and co-founder of Imaginative Inquiry said simply, "Resilience is seeing opportunity in adversity."

Next, I turned to the larger world of work to explore community resilience. Easier to define, perhaps, is a *working community*. Hive Networks, a company focused on the uses of technology for collaborations, supplies the following definition for a working community on its website:

> A working community is a collection of individuals that unite around a common passion and relentless focus to improve outcomes for a particular population. Members of a working community commit to sharing data, experience, and skills to design, develop and implement improvements inside and outside the clinical [work] setting.
>
> (Hive Networks 2022)

This definition holds up as meaningful and concise for the purposes of this book, with the modification that the focus is *teaching* communities. It embodies many of the attributes educators noted in what the term *teaching community* means to them. But it is missing *resilience*. So what makes a working or teaching community resilient?

The RAND Corporation defines *community resilience* as "a measure of the sustained ability of a community to utilize available resources to respond to, withstand, and recover from adverse situations" (Rand Corporation 2021).

In a school, the challenges arrive daily and come in varying sizes, from minor conflicts that can be resolved in a conversation, to acts of violence, to global pandemics. School violence and culture wars have affected schools for many years, and in varying degrees depending on geography and demographics. However, in the 21st century, mass school shootings, political control, and the COVID-19 pandemic have made these ubiquitous and frequent. In accordance with RAND's research on resilient communities, the schools included in this book have faced these challenges with resolve and cohesiveness by using the attributes of resilient communities and the strategies of teaching communities.

For insight into organizational resilience factors, I turned to Karen Reivich, from the University of Pennsylvania, who studies human resilience and is coauthor, with Andrew Shatté, of *The Resilience Factor: 7 Keys to Finding Your Inner Strength*

TABLE 2.1 Reivich and Shatte's *The Resilience Factor: 7 Keys to Finding Your Inner Strength and Overcoming Life's Hurdles*. This Table illustrates how Reivitch and Shatte's Seven Resilience Factors Play Out in Schools

Reivich and Shatté's Seven Resilience Factors	*How the Seven Resilience Factors Look in Schools*
Resilient individuals ...	**Resilient teaching communities ...**
Identify adversities, beliefs, and consequences;	Identify adversities the school is facing, uncover long-standing beliefs about the origins of those adversities, and debate the consequences of adhering to those beliefs;
Avoid common thinking traps that stop them from seeing reality as it is;	Examine their thinking, avoiding traps such as "jumping to conclusions, mind-reading, or catastrophizing," examine their thinking and welcome diversity of all kinds, including diverse perspectives;
Detect icebergs or hidden beliefs;	Share and acknowledge hidden beliefs and biases that could get in the way of inclusive practices, collaborations and innovations;
Challenge beliefs;	Challenge how "things have always been done" and are willing to go more deeply into problem-solving and change;
Put things in perspective;	Put challenges/conflicts in perspective, take the big-picture view, identify and focus on the mission and aspirations of the school;
Are calm and focused;	Build mindfulness into the daily life and practices of the faculty and students;
Apply real-time resilience.	Build mechanisms for responding, adjusting, and adapting to real-world crises and change.

and Overcoming Life's Hurdles. The seven resilience factors that Reivich and Shatté have identified are critical to personal resilience. In translating these factors for the school setting, I found them to have interesting ties to the seven attributes of resilient teaching communities (see Table 2.1) and have woven them into the text as the connections present themselves.

Resilience and Change

Despite our wishes and efforts, the damages of the pandemic are still being felt, and this is likely to continue for some time.

All students missed instruction and development in essential academic, executive function, and social skills, and some essential shifts in our collective perspective on the value and purpose of education took place that seems intractable. Students attending college in the aftermath of the pandemic missed a significant amount of high school teaching and learning, as well as social engagement and development. Students who were in first and second grade during the pandemic missed essential and foundational instruction in literacy and mathematics. Students, caregivers, schoolteachers, and staff have been through a trauma and a transformation. Piloting all students to a ready-to-learn state is taking ingenuity and commitment. While some schools are revising what school needs to look and feel like, "back to normal" seems to be the goal of most schools coming out of the pandemic. Meanwhile, a treasure trove of innovations, program development, and interventions that began to be developed during the pandemic remains unplumbed, and the opportunity to rethink and reimagine education is being squandered. Among these innovations is rethinking the role of teacher.

In a recent study by the Pew Research Center, 71% of teachers say, "teachers themselves don't have enough influence over what's taught in public schools in their area" (Lin et al. 2024). Leader participants find that when teachers are operating in a resilient teaching community in which challenges are faced together, they are no longer siloed in their classrooms with students. This community structure allows them to think interdependently, to discover concrete solutions to problems with their colleagues, and formulate cohesive policies, norms, and expectations of the whole community to support the kids. This approach to problem-solving as a contributor to resilience extends to the demands that teachers face as parents, caregivers, and community members. "Working in a team and meeting daily, we all have to be resilient," said Kelyn Snyder, a social studies teacher at Goff Middle School in East Greenbush, New York.

> We all have our things happening at home—the caregivers, the bus drivers, the teachers—and we are empathizing with each other. We all work together and

are flexible with each other and pivot when something isn't working. Flexibility is being ready for unexpected changes, circumstances, contexts, a student's schedule, big things or small things. And then we need to be as proactive as we can.

Resilient teaching communities rely on a deep well of collaboration and connection. That well is filled through an ease of interaction, a strong sense of interdependence and common purpose, and leadership that is engaged in supporting the vitality of the teaching community. In reflecting on what makes a working or teaching community resilient, Emmy Reiver, a middle school teacher at the Center School in Manhattan, replied: "I'd say a group of teachers who don't keep things to themselves. A group of people who are comfortable with each other, who care about each other. A group of people you feel secure around at the workplace."

While teachers themselves may choose to build relationships with other teachers that are collaborative, supportive, and/or social, the degree to which they do this will depend on the culture the leadership creates. I have spent time in schools in which leaders conquer through division and competition, and in which teachers are siloed and suspicious. And I have worked in, led, and for this book, studied schools in which the school leaders very purposefully bring people together. These are the visible and supportive leaders who are invitational and engaged.

Part 2

The Visible and Supportive Leader: Actively Cultivating Resilient Teaching Communities

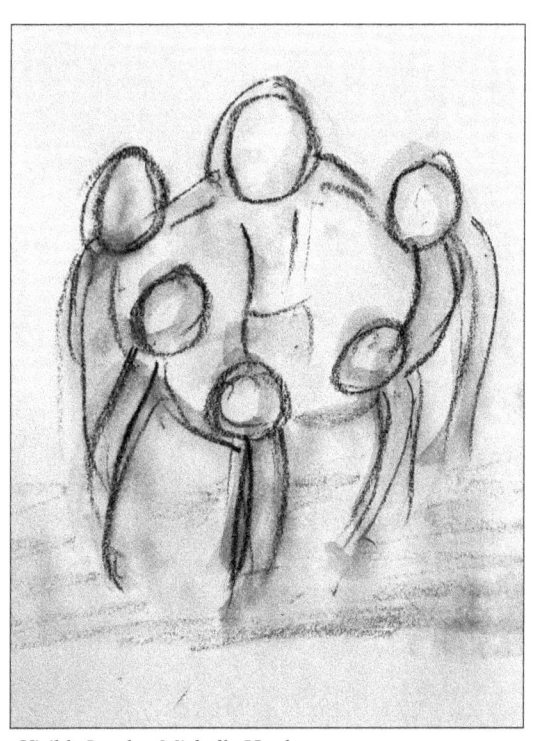

Illustration. The Visible Leader. Michelle Hughes.

3
Visible Leaders Growing and Sustaining Resilient Teaching Communities

> Visibility is a core value. My goal is to be in the office as little as possible and be out in classrooms, the hallways, drop off and pick up and on the playground. This allows me to build relationships across campus.
> – Assistant Principal Rusty Ito, Montecito Union Elementary

All school leaders—whether a team leader, department head, division head, teacher-director, principal, or superintendent—play a seminal role in the cultivation of a resilient teaching community. In conversations with every level of educator, interviewees observed that a visible and engaged leader makes all of the attributes of a resilient teaching community sustainable. This is borne out in the research. School leaders are essential to the *conditions* in which the teacher is teaching and are a factor in the *impact* that the teacher's instruction has on students. We can't really talk meaningfully about the impacts of a resilient teaching community on teaching and learning without considering the effects of the leadership under which the community is working.

Richard Strozzi-Heckler, founder of the Strozzi Institute and author of *The Leadership Dojo: Build Your Foundation as an Exemplary Leader*, surveyed multiple corporations, institutions, and military groups, asking "What are the character values most essential to exemplary leadership?" and he discovered the following:

> Honesty, accountability, integrity, vision, commitment, empathy, courage, trustworthiness, and self control showed up time and again as the hallmarks of a leader. ... these attributes have long been distinguished as the cornerstones of exemplary leadership.
> (Strozzi-Heckler 2007)

Indeed, none of these characteristics are surprising, and readers will find they *show up* in different ways in the many conversations throughout the book. Though these attributes can be learned and adopted, they are observable and seemingly natural to the leaders with whom I spoke. Big-picture, long-view thinkers, they understand the importance of continuity and longevity, and they display most or all of Reivich and Shatte's seven resilience factors as described. They are able to put problems in perspective and will seek to collaborate with others to establish and work toward long-term goals. Because these leaders have made the effort to build relationships and trust, the teachers they work with say they are willing to give of their time and energy for the greater good of their schools.

The Difference a Visible and Engaged Leader Makes

At the end of one of those long hard days as a school leader, I sometimes wondered what I accomplished that day, and in more difficult moments, what difference I was making. These are feelings that leaders know well. But, in their sweeping review of the research on the impact of school leadership on student learning, Kenneth Leithwood, Karen Seashore Louis, Stephen Anderson, and Kyla Wahlstrom note that leaders come second only to teachers in influence on student learning. Good leaders, they found, create the environment in which effective teaching and learning can happen.

How do high-quality leaders achieve this impact?

By setting directions—charting a clear course that everyone understands, establishing high expectations and using data to track progress and performance.

By developing people—providing teachers and others in the system with the necessary support and training to succeed.

And by making the organization work—ensuring that the entire range of conditions and incentives in districts and schools fully supports rather than inhibits teaching and learning.

(Leithwood et al. 2004)

Over the course of my years as a school leader, the more visible I was, the more available I was to teachers and students for relationship building. Though time taken during the day for "people work" meant saving the "operations work" for the end of the day, much time and energy was saved in other kinds of interventions and reconnaissance. The payoff in trust building was profound. This shift in time usage and priorities can be monumental, but also critical in growing collective resilience. In fact, leaders who undertake a change from the traditional hierarchical model of leadership to leading resilient teaching communities are hovering between first- and second-order changes.

In first-order change, leaders engage employees in mechanical adjustments such as schedule modifications or the introduction of a new curriculum. First-order changes can be highly specific, affecting few people or programs, or they can be more sweeping, such as the current emergence of the "science of reading" movement, which puts forth ample research to support the teaching of phonemic and phonic skills. In the training and implementation of science of reading programs, whole curricula are being called into question, debunked, and replaced. However sweeping this change is to curricula and approaches, it does not require transformation of operational structures, mission, or culture—it is not second-order change (Marzano 2010).

In second-order change, entities undergo or undertake a full reckoning of identity, purpose, and/or structure. Second-order change in education rarely happens without an emergent event, such as the COVID-19 pandemic. Yet even the pandemic did not permanently alter our presumptions about what makes effective teaching and learning in most schools. In fact, many schools, in an effort to return to "normal," seem to have thrown out the ingenuity, innovations, and rethinking that emerged during the pandemic. The ruts we travel on the road to educating our populace are so deep that it is easy to yield control of the steering wheel to their well-worn routes and patterns.

The education establishment has long used first-order change methods to attempt to address conditions that required something closer to second-order change, thus those solutions do not tend to be enduring. But when an entity—a company, organization, or school—is facing a crisis of the magnitude we see today in the numbers of educators leaving the profession, something close to second-order change is called for. I say "close to" because the *what*—the fundamental premise of a school to educate—is not in question, but the *how,* the mission, is.

Psynet, a corporate consultancy, makes the following distinction between first and second-order change:

> With few exceptions, most organizational change is a response to either a crisis or an opportunity. The organization then decides whether or not to implement a first or second order change. A first order change is easier and requires adapting to the circumstances. For example, rearranging our office space to increase distance between workers is a first order change. In this case, the seminal event is more of a nuisance.
>
> Second order change happens when the seminal event causes an organization to question its identity. [The organization's members] experience a feeling that

their values and purpose no longer make sense in the context of the event.

(Psynet Group 2024)

The prospect of cultivating a resilient teaching community asks leaders to rethink the values, relationships, roles, and structures of their school and lead fundamental changes to invigorate and engage teachers and, ultimately, students. Donald Thomas, in his 1973 book *The Schools Next Time: Explorations in Educational Sociology*, framed the obstacles to change that schools, teachers, and leaders were facing even then: "Organizational change involving people and their social arrangements is never simple, particularly if such people consider their traditional structures virtually sacred, and also if the tools for modification are not yet honed to precision" (Thomas 1973). The difficulties in overcoming such obstacles often fall to the leader. As education researcher and consultant Robert Marzano warns, "The leader has got to be able to live through the tough times" (Marzano 2010).

Teachers broadly shared the perspective that a visible, consistent, and honest presence of a leader was key to building trust between teachers and leaders. Karen Nichols, high school math teacher and administrator at Oakwood Friends in Poughkeepsie, New York, observed,

> If you don't have a principal or leader who is walking around, who is saying things that show they know you as a person, who asks about your day, you don't build those micro moments of trust; you have to have those, and they are cumulative. Those busy behind-doors-in-a-meeting leaders create a sense of distrust." In their, chapter "How leadership influences student learning.

In the Wallace Foundation's *Learning from Leadership Project: Review of Research,* authors Kenneth Leithwood, Karen Seashore Louis, Stephen Anderson, and Kyla Wahlstrom affirm this observation:

> Superintendents and other district-level leaders in academically successful school districts convey a strong belief in the capacity of school system personnel to achieve high standards of learning for all students, and high standards of teaching and leadership from all instructional and support personnel. This is marked by a willingness to identify poor performance (student, teacher, school) and other obstacles to success, to accept responsibility and to seek solutions.
>
> (Leithwood et al. 2004)

When leaders trust teachers, and teachers feel *seen* as professionals, they collaborate and share decision-making with teachers and set essential conditions for fostering resilient teaching communities. Many educators work toward these operational cornerstones at great risk to themselves, believing these practices are essential not only to the well-being of teachers and students but also to encouraging high performance in both groups. Power sharing means giving up some control in exchange for sharing the weight of the work. Leaders who take this risk know the traditional hierarchy of schools has not been a catalyst for change. The recognition of this may be one of the enduring effects of the pandemic, forced by the loss of teachers, on the one hand, and the loss of status of the teaching profession that is reducing applicants to education programs, on the other. There is ample evidence that each of the seven attributes of a resilient teaching community has a significant and positive impact on teaching and learning—making cultivating such a community well worth the risk.

> **Reflect. Act.**
>
> *I take care of my faculty first, so they can take care of who matters most.*
> – Crystal Thorpe, principal, Fishers Junior High School, Fishers, Indiana

Visible and engaged team, department, division, school, and district leaders are essential to the educational excellence that comes with cultivating a collaborative and connected faculty. In cultivating each of the seven attributes of a resilient teaching community, the leader must proceed with a certain amount of confidence in the process and the people they lead.

Over the years of working with students who struggle, I sought a visual that would capture the components of confidence and demystify what it takes to feel confident in our work. Kids often feel that their peers are just born confident, or that confidence is a mask one puts on. Now I use this three-legged stool in the work I do with kids and adults to show that confidence is built from recognizable and attainable states of being: clarity, ability, and completion.

At the end of Chapters 4–7, you have the opportunity to reflect in a way that can lead to positive action. You are offered the opportunity to reflect on and devise actions to build trust, celebrate belonging, institute collaboration and shared decision-making, and implement ongoing professional growth, using the stages of attaining clarity: what you hope to do and why; assessing abilities: Who on your team and faculty have which strengths they bring to the process; and completion: How will you move forward? How will you know you've achieved the beginning of a lasting change?

The first leg of the confidence stool is gaining **clarity** on expectations, methods, means, and goals. Skills, knowledge, experience, disposition, and openness to ongoing learning make up a person's **ability** to accomplish a task. Knowing who possesses these traits in which areas allows one to pick the right person or group of people for the right task (Figure 3.1).

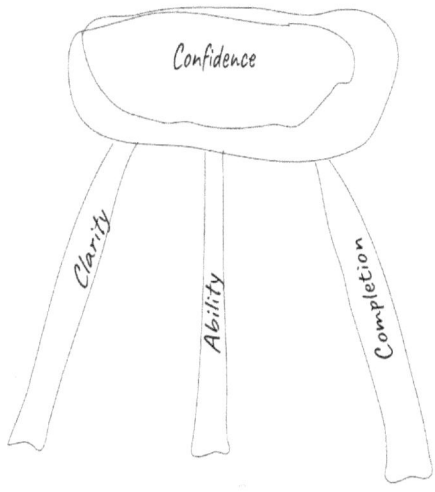

FIGURE 3.1 Confidence Stool, Original by Michelle Hughes.

In *The Speed of Trust*, Stephen Covey III says that in order to trust others, we need to feel they not only share the same intentions but have the ability to carry out the task. Assessing the individual capacities of faculty and staff is not a pass-fail endeavor; it is about what is the right work for each person, in the area where they can offer the most, and colleagues and students can gain the most.

Completion is less defined in the work of cultivating a resilient teaching community, as ongoing maintenance and growth opportunities are part and parcel to such a community. However, when change begins to take root, as each of the attributes becomes part and parcel of the experience of leadership, teachers, staff, and students, a sense of completion can be felt. This builds confidence in the process and product.

Habits of Mind

In the process of change, it can be helpful to have a framework and common language for the ways of thinking and the approaches we use. As a practitioner of the Habits of Mind, I offer the Habits of Mind chart below as a way of describing and cataloging strengths, and clarifying goals. More information on the history and foundations of the Habits of Mind can be found at https://www.habitsofmindinstitute.org/ (Figure 3.2).

Visible Leaders and Resilient Teaching Communities ♦ 27

Thinking About Your Thinking (Metacognition)
Know your Knowing!
Being aware of your own thoughts, strategies, feelings and actions and their effects on others.

Persisting
Stick to it!
Persevering with a task through to completion; remaining focused. Searching for ways to reach your goal when stuck. Not giving up.

Managing Impulsivity
Take your time!
Thinking before acting; remaining calm, thoughtful and deliberative.

Striving for Accuracy
Check it again!
Doing your best. Setting high standards. Fact checking and finding ways to improve.

Listening with Understanding and Empathy
Understand others!
Devoting mental energy to another person's thoughts and ideas. Making an effort to perceive another's point of view and emotions.

Thinking Flexibly
Look at it another way!
Being able to change perspectives; generating alternatives, considering options.

Questioning and Posing Problems
How do you know?
Having a questioning attitude; knowing what data are needed & developing questioning strategies to produce those data. Finding problems to solve.

Thinking Interdependently
Work together!
Working with and learning from others in reciprocal situations. Teamwork.

Thinking & Communicating with Clarity and Precision
Be clear!
Striving for accurate communication in both written and oral form; avoiding over-generalizations, distortions, deletions and exaggerations.

Applying Past Knowledge to New Situations
Use what you learn!
Accessing prior knowledge; transferring knowledge beyond the situation in which it was learned.

Gathering Data Through All Senses
Use your natural pathways!
Paying attention to the world around you. Gathering data through all the senses: Sight, Sound, Smell, Taste, and Touch.

Creating, Imagining, and Innovating
Try a different or new way!
Generating possibilities, playing with new ideas.

Taking Responsible Risks
Venture out!
Being adventuresome; living on the edge of your competence.

Finding Humor
Laugh a little!
Finding the whimsical, incongruous and unexpected. Being able to laugh at one's self.

Responding with Wonderment and Awe
Become intrigued!
Finding the world awesome, mysterious and being intrigued with phenomena and beauty.

Remaining Open to Continuous Learning
Learn throughout your lifetime!
Having humility and admitting when you don't know and are curious to find out. Resisting complacency.

FIGURE 3.2 Habits of Mind Graphic.

4

Build Trust

Through all the questions you are asking in this research, the word that comes to me is trust. You can't do any of these things if there is no trust. If the head of school can create an atmosphere of trust, it ripples down.

– Doris Gonzalez Easton, associate head of school and colleague

Jeff Simons, superintendent of schools in East Greenbush, New York, concurs. He takes the role of trust to the next level of the hierarchy. "Within the ranks of school leadership," he says, "a trusting relationship between the superintendent and the board is very important. That trickles down into the classroom as well." Positive relationships between school boards or boards of trustees and the school leaders they appoint lead to continuity and longevity of the leadership, and this has positive outcomes for schools. In such a setting, leaders model listening to disparate voices, and teachers share their practices and work with others for the benefit of the whole. In building trust there must be a willingness on all parts to be vulnerable, which can be somewhat perilous in many schools and school systems in which fault finding and blame is endemic—a reason many do not undertake this work.

"My goal is to always follow up with any agreement, request, or conversation," Rusty Ito said. "This might be connecting with a student or family, getting an additional student desk, setting up a meeting, or simply dropping by the classroom to support a staff member." Rusty is an assistant principal at Montecito Union Elementary School, in Montecito, California; he began as a teacher twelve years ago and moved into administration four years ago. He believes his teaching background factors into the trust he has built with the teachers over his twelve years at the school. As a leader who began as a teacher of many years, I connect with Rusty's observation. In fact, many teachers expressed to me the importance of a school leader understanding the work teachers do and the lives they lead.

In his book *The Advantage*, Patrick Lencioni, a prolific writer and researcher on how teams work, writes that vulnerability "is not going to happen if the leader of the team, whether a CEO, department head, pastor, or principal, does not go first" (Lencioni 2012). The word *vulnerable*, from Latin roots, means "the ability to be wounded." Leaders can find trust too great a risk to their own standing. What if the teacher does not perform their duties to community standards? What if the teacher takes a creative risk with curriculum and it flops? What if teachers present challenges in a shared decision-making setting? Will the leader be seen as weak and ineffective?

In the hierarchy of a school, the school leader must trust the teacher to be effective, knowledgeable, responsible, engaged, and mission-driven. The teacher then needs to trust that the leader will provide support, resources, time, and attention for them to meet the expectations of the leader. In *The Speed of Trust*, Stephen Covey explores the elements and importance of trust and what trust looks like. Inextricable from the establishment of trust is the willingness to be vulnerable. In schools, to climb out on the limb of trust, we need to believe in the intentions and abilities of others to effectively carry out the collectively agreed-upon mission and to support one another in the endeavor. Whether school leader or teacher, each holds these expectations for the other. Covey breaks trust down into four essential elements: integrity, intention, capability, and results (Covey 2018).

Our integrity, or how well we have integrated our values into our thoughts and actions, is consciously and intuitively observed by all who depend on us, work with us, and live with us. Actions that consistently conflict with what we say we believe in, care about, and value will call our trustworthiness into question. Covey goes further to say intentions count. What we aim to do, try to do, and focus on matters, even when things don't work out. If one is perceived to have integrity and honorable intentions, there is a greater chance one will not lose trust when things don't work out (Covey 2018). This plays out directly with our students' learning and behavior. When trust is modelled by school leaders and then returned by teachers, positive change can happen as trust ripples down to students and families.

Mary Ellen Tomson, a former middle school history teacher at the Albany Academies, thought back on changes in leadership that led to positive changes in practices.

> There was a period when we were really struggling with our eighth-grade students. But, under a new leader we shifted practices. Once the kids knew they would be heard, they worked with us. Because they were trusting us, they bought in, and then parents bought in.

Integrity and good intentions will go only so far, however, if both parties—leaders and followers—do not feel the other is *capable* of doing the thing they intend. They will not trust each other to do the final thing, and that is to achieve results. In any dynamic, whether parent–child, boss–worker, or administrator–teacher, if one party continuously promises what it does not have the capability to deliver, they will lose trust.

Building and giving trust hinges on knowing and respecting each other's histories, priorities, and styles, and believing everyone on the team has the intentions, knowledge, and expertise to do what they need to do (Lencioni 2012). Trust is just one of five behaviors that Lencioni identifies that cohesive teams must establish to build a healthy organization. However, it is by far the most important one because it is the foundation for the others. Simply stated, it makes teamwork possible.

The Role of Teachers in Cultivating Resilient Teaching Communities

When leaders build a culture of trust that permeates the relationships between and among cohorts of professionals. In my conversations with teachers, they expressed the importance of trust within the teaching ranks to take creative risks and be responsive to what's happening in the classroom. Feeling your team has confidence in your skills and decision-making, leads to feelings of competence and confidence. In her role as Response to Intervention coordinator in the East Greenbush School District, Lisa Mahar collaborates with and trains many teachers, giving her a bird's-eye view from which she has observed that "teachers are more likely to take creative risks and feel less isolated when they feel trusted." She sees the merits of trust generating wide-ranging impacts. "When I feel trusted, I bring this back to the teachers I work with. Everyone feels supported, and they work together, so when students or teachers have a need, it doesn't matter, it is all hands on deck."

Teachers play a critical role in creating a culture of collaboration and community. Forcing themselves out of the isolation of their classrooms and into the life of the school as a whole can be challenging, even as collaboration and engagement encourage belonging, growth, and change. Jackie Katzen describes this as,

> The feeling that you can go to virtually any one of your colleagues with something that you are trying to work out, without concern that ego will be involved, is huge. And [so is] being able to decide which person has the most advanced skill in the area that I specifically need the support in, and knowing that I would always make time to be available to anyone else.

Mentorship is critical to the inclusion and development of new teachers, among whom attrition rates are high. As a new public school teacher, I was fortunate to work in highly collaborative teams. Being among veteran teachers who were willing to support and teach me enriched my experience, attenuated the isolation, and made me a better teacher. "When I think about it," former middle school history teacher Mary Ellen Tomson mused,

> what made it [Albany Academies] feel like a community was that I always had a mentor. I always had people I learned from. I know that I need that leadership of vision and perspective. A lot of that resilience came from feelings that I was led well, and that my peers were also being led well. There were enough people that were moving forward for the kids.

School administrators who value teacher-to-teacher relationships such as mentorship, make time for it. At Mission Vista High School in California, layers of connection and mentorship happen through grade-level and discipline-based Professional Learning Communities, in which teachers engage in building curriculum or programs over a period of time. These are on the calendar, which establishes Vista's commitment to collaboration.

> Our principal does things like all general information is shared in an email, so at meetings information takes only ten minutes, the rest of the time [the focus is on] discussion and action with an opportunity to collectively engage with each other in the work. It is a strategic thing they do to show teachers how important the work is we are doing together.

said Will Salley.

In building and supporting strong collegial relationships, leaders become part of the engine of ongoing collaborative work that teachers are doing. The relationships that are built over time allow trust to grow between teachers and school leaders, which humanizes the work environment. This reciprocity might be a factor in the longevity of the leader in a school or district.

"We hear very frequently, we have permission to fail," Michelle Daum, from Mission Vista High School reflects. "Try it—if it's not working, we are here to support you. Our principal, one of his strengths is empathy, and he's very good at listening, doing empathy interviews with students and really listening."

When I became head of school, there were moments when I would step back and secretly contemplate the most terrifying notion that thirty-five teachers were in classrooms *trying things*. I understood it for what it was—the worry that something would come back to me I didn't anticipate—and I suppressed the momentary desire to reign everyone in. This syndrome faded over time, as I got to know my faculty really well and got to know their classrooms, curricula, and signature projects through our collaborations. Having deep knowledge about the teaching and learning happening in the classrooms, having positive and collaborative relationships with the teachers, these were the underpinning of my trust in them. In other words, we need to build trust on strong foundations.

"The school leaders are in our classrooms at least once a month," Michelle Daum shared as an example of the supportive and collaborative relationships between leadership and teachers in her district. The intimacy and trust leaders develop with teachers around the work happening in the classrooms are key to the creative and academic freedoms the teachers enjoy. In my former school and in the participating schools I visited, this trust is rooted in the collaboration in which all parties were constantly engaged.

> **Reflect. Act. Trust.**
>
> *You have to ensure you don't have a 'gotcha culture.' The leader has to model it in conversations in which they take an inquiry approach, being a thinking partner with teachers.*
>
> – Ross Hogan, Principal

Step 1: Attaining Clarity

Building a culture of trust can't be done alone. It happens one person at a time, with each person possessing their own *speed of trust* based on experience and disposition. Yet, through consistency with each person and across the community, trust seems to happen all at once. When trust is established, teachers feel freed up to exercise autonomy, to co-create in groups, and to trust colleagues and students.

Reflect: I want to cultivate trust in the Teaching Community.	Act: What will I continue to do or start doing?
What do I need to know to trust teachers to make decisions, create curriculum, and build student and family relationships?	
Have I built relationships with the faculty, one by one? Do I have a clear sense of their whole person?	
Do I have a clear picture of the faculty dynamics? Am I actively engaged in creating an inclusive teaching environment?	
What are clear and potential obstacles to the endeavor to establish trust? How will I surmount these?	

Notes:

Step 2: Assessing Ability

In any endeavor, it is critical that we understand the strengths and challenges we and others bring to the table.

Reflect: I want to cultivate trust in the Teaching Community.	Act: What steps will I take to assess my own skills and abilities, and those that teachers and staff possess, in building trust?
What strengths do I bring to the process of building trust? How am I trustworthy?	What habits of mind will I cultivate in order to lead on trust?
What am I willing to risk in modeling trust?	What skills and routines do I need to build in order to cultivate a culture of trust?
Have I spent enough time in classrooms and in one-on-one meetings to gain a true sense of each person's style, strengths, and growing edges?	How will I reprioritize my habits and time to be present in classrooms, hallways, and in conversations with teachers?
Am I asking the right people for the right work?	Rethink how and from whom I ask tasks to be led/completed.

Step 3: Achieving Completion

While building and maintaining trust is an ongoing endeavor. In this case, completion really means a transformation has taken place in which trust is offered, felt, and shared.

Reflect: What does completion look like?	Act

How will I begin?	Who will be my seed group? What makes these people trustworthy?
How will trusting faculty and staff shift my outlook?	How will my work change? How will I use my time differently?
What will a sense of being trusted allow teachers and staff to achieve in their work?	What personal attributes do they possess that make them the right person?
How will this trickle down to students and their school experience?	What are the qualities of their relationships in the teaching community?

5

Forge a Community of Belonging

To deepen my understanding of the role of belonging in schools, I turned to David Levine, founding director of the Teaching Empathy Institute in Stone Ridge, New York, who writes and conducts research and workshops around the country on empathy and belonging. In his *Field Guide to a School of Belonging*, he writes,

> When school leaders seek to integrate social and emotional learning as a critical component of a school's culture, they enhance success through sensitivity and inclusivity. School staff need to be given the opportunity to have authentic and meaningful **exploratory** conversations with their colleagues as a social and emotional (SEL) community of practice….
>
> (Levine 2020)

In our commitment to building resilient communities in our schools, many schools think about students and skip right past teachers. But, a sense of belonging in the workplace is consistently observed and felt by participating teachers, broadly through school culture and individually through day-to-day interactions. Lauren DeGeorgia, dean of students at Albany Academies, observes the small things that bolster belonging in her teaching community: "The way we eat together, hold the door for each other, say hello—the little things matter, and everyone knows your name."

In a post-COVID review of the job satisfaction surveys of teachers and principals, entitled "Restoring Teacher and Principal Well-Being Is an Essential Step for Rebuilding Schools," researchers found:

> Many district and school leaders already work hard to build supportive environments and should build on their success. Leaders who have not made adult relationships a priority could consider transferring the strategies they use to build positive student-staff relationships to focus on adults. Leaders might also consider actions that could foster camaraderie among staff—such as intentional opportunities for social interactions—to build positive relationships among different groups of staff.
>
> (Steiner et al. 2022)

When I asked teachers at Manhattan's Center School about what conditions at the school support the development of resilience in their teaching community, middle school teacher Emmy Reiver pointed toward acceptance, feeling that the ability to be authentic was key to her ability to fully participate in the life of the school. "Ms. Schwartz [founder-director of the school] lets us be ourselves wholeheartedly, down to the clothing we wear; there is no judgment." In fact, in *The Leadership Dojo*, Richard Strozzi-Heckler cites a Gallup poll that surveyed more than a billion people worldwide about work and found that four out of five people were dissatisfied at their job sites because they could not bring their full selves to their work (Strozzi-Heckler 2007). I looked into these findings and found that when people could not bring their full selves to work, "regardless of work location (including fully remote employees), organizational satisfaction, clarity of expectations, opportunities to do what you do best, and feeling connected to the organization's mission or purpose declined substantially" (Biron 2023).

"In building relationships with staff, students, and families some of the most important conversations are focused on topics outside of school. Getting to know their interests, history, and who they are as people is critical." Rusty Ito reflects. In teaching, being one's full self is critical to one's teaching practice allowing one to engage authentically with students, to make sound decisions, and to build meaningful curriculum. These are difficult to accomplish in schools where teachers and students cannot be their full selves. Sitting together over lunch with Michelle Daum and Will Salley at Mission Vista High School, they talked about feeling trusted to make decisions in their classrooms. "It is part of what makes the magic here in Vista. We feel appreciated and known."

On Teacher Evaluation

As a byproduct of the nationwide high stakes assessment and standards movements many states designed teacher evaluation systems that were tied to students' performance on tests. As an inclusive teacher, with a quarter of our team's students having learning disabilities, we knew that our aggregate assessment scores would be lower than that of our general education colleagues.' While we had many authentic assessments of work in the classroom to demonstrate student progress, in addition to tenure, we had peers who feared for their jobs. These teacher evaluation systems have been under attack, and modified slightly, but the message is clear: Your value as a teacher has been reduced to narrow quantitative measures.

In her chapter, "Disruptive Engagement: Daring to Rehumanize Education and Work," in her book *Daring Greatly*, Brene Brown describes an organization in which "respect and dignity are held at the highest values. … Empathy is a valued asset, accountability is an expectation rather than an exception, and the primal human need for belonging is not used as leverage or social control" (Brown 2012). *Sitting beside* personnel or pupils in the process of giving feedback connotes the leader or teacher is on the side of the person being assessed. Interestingly, the Latin root for the word *assess* is *assidere*, which means "to sit beside." Thus, Brown asks, "How would engagement change if leaders *sat down next to folks* [my italics] and said, 'Thank you for your contributions. *Here's* how you are making a difference. *This* issue is getting in the way of your growth'" (Brown 2012).

In the participating schools I visited, teachers feel seen in the specificity of the feedback and support they receive from their leaders. Stephen Haff, teacher of English and drama at Poughkeepsie Day School, put it this way:

> It's wonderful when appreciation comes from someone knowing your work, when someone has been in your classroom or has had extended conversations about pedagogy. When those folks see you, that is so rewarding and sustaining. But when you get pro forma praise as a substitute for genuine daily support, it's discouraging. Thanks won't fill the car or put food in the fridge, but the right thanks will help me carry on.

Jackie Katzen, former teacher and school administrator, listed two "primary conditions for leaders who are fostering belonging in a resilient teaching community: having an open door, and having it be clear that the head of school is someone for people to go to without fear of reprisal." Expanding on the second point, she stressed the importance of "leadership standing up for teachers and being open with teachers when there is work to be done on their part when something has to shift."

Fishers Junior High School teachers shared their thoughts with me about the circumstances unfolding from the pandemic.

> Everybody is on the same page, accepting this is not where we want to be, or where we'll be five years from now, but we are here right now, and we are freed up to say, 'Okay, I'm going to address what's happening right now'.

Joy Frush reflected. "Without micromanaging," Jenna Pyle adds, Fishers Junior High principal Crystal Thorpe "talks to us about how we can do things better, but she also asks questions like, 'how can I support you?'"

Imagine if every teacher and child felt this way at school. As you have read, the Center School works hard at creating a culture of belonging. This responsibility begins with the leader, but rests on every teacher and student's shoulder to continually reinforce.

Step 1: Attaining Clarity

David Levine, director of the Teaching Empathy Institute, and author of *The Field Guide to a School of Belonging*, and *A Year of Belonging*, defines belonging as "Affiliation and Attachment to the group and school community." Affiliation comes from the latin *affiliare*-to adopt, with filius meaning son and filia meaning daughter. Though we rarely think of affiliation that way now, to feel truly affiliated means to feel like family.

> **Reflect. Act. Celebrate Connection.**
>
> "We show kids that if we can be ourselves, so can you," Emmy Reiver told me. "These kids are so special, are so unapologetic and unafraid to be who they are. We foster a community where people are unafraid to be themselves."
> – Middle School Teacher, The Center School

According to this definition, on a scale of 1–10, where is your school on the trajectory toward Belonging?

Teachers: Not present — Just Beginning — Amongst some groups, but exclusionary — most feel they belong — universally felt

Students: Not present — Just Beginning — Amongst some groups, but exclusionary — most feel they belong — universally felt

How do you know?

Cultivating belonging happens through the seeing and valuing school members for their strengths, talents, dispositions, knowledge, and expertise. Belonging thrives in an environment in which diversity of all kinds is seen as a strength for the community and where divergent points of view are invited.

Steps 2 and 3

Trust, collaboration, shared decision-making, and opportunities for ongoing Professional Growth are attributes that cultivate a sense of belonging. For each attribute, you will engage different people to comprise your Seed Group for cultivating that attribute. Your Seed Group is composed of those you choose to start with in each endeavor. Participation in a seed group should not be an exclusionary device, but one that each teacher or staff member looks forward to because the specific work of that group speaks to them, intrigues them, or they possess knowledge and skills suited to the work.

6

Provide Opportunities for Ongoing Professional Growth

When I first arrived at the Center School, I was led into the front office, where I thought the director, Elaine Schwartz would be. But Elaine had moved her desk into a busy computer room, which, in many ways, is a hub for the school. Kids and teachers are in and out for classes or academic support, and people stop in regularly to talk with Elaine. She is in the mix, moment to moment, day to day. In fact, none of the school leaders I visited were found in their offices (Figure 6.1).

FIGURE 6.1 Ongoing Professional Learning.

DOI: 10.4324/9781003644149-8

At participating schools, chosen for the attributes they share with resilient teaching communities, I heard over and over from teachers about the freedom they had to experiment that would not fly in most places. Their school leaders shared the conviction that teachers have to be allowed to "try things" and that this practice is "the key to growth." Leaders of resilient teaching communities cultivate teachers who experience and bounce back from challenging situations, lessons that fail, and unpredictable conditions—and provide them with a community to support and bolster them. "Respecting the work that teachers do, mindful of the experience they have, and the priorities they set," said Crystal Thorpe, principal of Fishers Junior High School in Fishers, Indiana, led her to *ask less* of her teachers in the 2023–24 school year. Most often, the best route to learning is to go more deeply into content rather than *cover* more, and Crystal had the courage to pursue this route in bringing her school back to standard after the losses sustained during the pandemic. Crystal explained, "I wanted to acknowledge the work teachers had done throughout the pandemic and focus on the initiatives *they* care about. As a result, they have come up with great programs that engage the whole school, parents as well!" This not only honored the teachers' experience through the pandemic but allowed them to exercise some autonomy in creating and innovating. In our conversation, we agreed that engagement is a key element of a resilient teaching community.

> You can learn about Crystal's thought processes in her *Education Week* article "Why One Principal Is Asking Her Staff to Do Less: How to Get Back to the Basics".
>
> (Thorpe 2022)

When school leaders engage with teachers in co-creating educational and culture-building programs they gain insight into the knowledge and strengths of their faculty, as well as areas for learning and growth. Kelyn Snyder described how

Superintendent Simons' approach to cultivating instructional leadership among his principals influences her teaching practice and encourages creative risk-taking in her school:

> There is the sense, 'I have never done this before.' And the principal [is] supportive, saying, 'Sure, try it, and see what happens,' and the parents are also behind this. It goes back to flexibility, [the idea that] if it does bomb, it's okay.

Kelyn added,

> I have experienced school leaders who have really gone [above and] beyond. When I say, 'I'm thinking of doing this,' they say, 'Do it! Try it!' They will get us the resources we need, and are in the thick of it with us. They are willing to get their hands dirty.

However, if biannual observations and evaluations are the only means by which school leaders come to know their teachers and their practices, they are seeing what is unfolding through a tiny window. Consistent and engaged leaders have regular conversations with their teachers and give frequent, constructive feedback. Principal Ross Hogan at the Duzine Elementary School in New Paltz, New York cautioned,

> You have to ensure you don't have a 'gotcha' culture. The leader has to model it in conversations in which they take an inquiry approach, being a thinking partner with teachers. When trying something new, saying, 'Don't worry, this is a pilot, and we are learning together.'

The keys to a leader's success with faculty have more to do with the integrity they bring to their relationships which creates openness between teachers and leaders to co-creating the schooling experience. High school English teacher Meagan Asenbauer describes, "We include them [school leaders]; they are in on everything. We invite them to be part of the conversation. They sit right at the table."

East Greenbush Central School District, East Greenbush, New York
Collaborative and Supportive Leadership

East Greenbush, New York, is located just east of the state capital, Albany, in the foothills of the Berkshires. The East Greenbush district comprises an elementary school, a middle school, and a high school; it was awarded "Top Workplace" by the *Albany Times Union* in 2018, 2019, and 2021.

Taking time out of a busy day, Jeff Simons, superintendent of schools, was easy to talk with and genuinely excited and moved by the work his teachers and school leaders do. In talking about what collaborative leadership looked like Jeff said, "I ask them, tell me where you want to go with this, what you need, and we'll find the resources."

In my follow-up conversations with teachers Kelyn Snyder, Lisa Mahar, and Meagan Asenbauer, they spoke to a common vision and an unusual level of trust and collaboration underlie the daily life of the school.

Lisa Mahar pointed out that having one's full self recognized means,

> being supported — not just professionally, but personally. So when we come to school, the teachers, the administrators, the bus drivers, the custodians, we want to know that we are coming to school not just to serve the students, but [we also want it to be known] that we have lives outside of school, that we are people.

Ongoing Professional Growth

The Institute for Habits of Mind was founded by Bena Kallick and Art Costa to disseminate and offer resources and professional development on the sixteen habits of mind identified through their years of research that are shown to undergird personal efficacy and fulfillment. Among the sixteen habits of mind Costa and Kallick identified in their research is to *remain open to continuous learning.* This *habit of mind* is a critical component of collaboration and growth as a teacher, yet remarkably undervalued in how we think about teachers as learners in our education system.

Learning is a high-risk endeavor; we feel exposed and vulnerable in the space between knowing and coming to know something new. Developmental psychologist Lev Vygotsky's well known theory of the "zone of proximal development"—the space between a learner's solo capabilities and the potential they can reach with guidance—is often referred to in discussions of student learning. But it describes a human dynamic by which adults are equally challenged. Brene Brown characterizes the zone of proximal development as *vulnerability*. To create a sense of safety for his teachers in taking on new knowledge or trying new strategies or curriculum, Spiro Gouras, the new head at Poughkeepsie Day School, often goes first:

> I like to share dilemmas and put out fires together. I don't mind showing vulnerability. Occasionally you can show that you are the ultimate person in charge, but it's OK to say, 'this is going on, and we need to figure this out.' You can get a bunch of ideas from people, and then they know that they were part of that input.

Collegial trust is gained in a multitude of ways in the work environment. In a profession in which roles are typically siloed, this takes effort, patience, and time. One way is through professional learning experiences, in which teachers are called upon to learn together in authentic ways, develop programs, and learn new skills. Moving forward on initiatives, tuning into current ideas and movements in education, and having exposure to the world of ideas are all possible through professional development. Schoolwide professional development can provide a rich opportunity for co-creation.

> Learning experiences go beyond the workshop format to include such things as teacher inter- visitations, demonstration lessons, in-class coaching and teams of teachers doing lesson study, curriculum planning and analysis of assessment data. Teacher development involves multi-year goals for instructional improvement (e.g., reading, mathematics) and increased school control over professional development (PD) decisions and resources in the context of district goals for improvement.
>
> (Leithwood et al.2004)

In our conversations and communications, leaders and teachers agreed that professional development resources are important. Tania de Rosier, a middle school English teacher drew a connection between healthy teacher-leader relationships and resources:

> An administrative community that cares about the well-being of its teachers fosters open communication and listens to what teachers need. Then they respond to those needs with appropriate support, education, or services to assist the teacher so she/he/they can do the best for their students.

Post-PD Follow-Up and Follow-Through

As we explored the topic of professional development and ongoing growth, when participating teachers reflected on the value of professional development it was often in the contrast between extemporaneous and planned teacher collaboration and learning. There was a general sense that professional development days were valuable only when they were relevant to the classroom, to a need, and had follow-up. Jeff Fisher made this comparison between structured professional development and faculty collaborative work and meetings:

> Professional development can feel kind of hit and run. I believe in agendas, and not every meeting needs to be a

therapy session. But we absolutely need those opportunities to just share with each other, not feel alone, to feel like someone understands.

Karen Nichols, of Oakwood Friends School in Poughkeepsie, reflected,

> When I think about in-service days, people usually come away with either a reaction of 'Wow, we did something new as a group and brainstormed a collective goal that we are ready to move forward on' or 'That was a stupid day.' But along with those kinds of days, there has to be follow-through and time and space for gatherings. When it doesn't happen, teachers become demoralized.

As a school leader, on days devoted to professional development, I was often surprised that consultants found it remarkable that I attended alongside the teachers. Some consultants felt disconcerted by my presence at first, while others felt supported. There were many reasons for my attendance, primary among them my ability to provide ongoing support, time, and structure for whatever content was being shared and to make the time needed for the integration process. Attending the sessions allowed me to gauge teachers' responses to the learning, assess what the next steps were and how I could support the changes that would be needed, or to begin to think about resources such changes would demand. As a small school on a tight budget, if we were spending time and money on professional development, it was because it was essential learning for us. I needed to be present and engaged in order to anticipate the resources required to activate and actualize that learning. However, giving that time was challenging with so many other demands on my plate. I was constantly weighing the cost-benefit analysis of attending professional development, and tried to find a balance between teaching and learning and operations.

Professional development is often a mechanism for making and managing change as a community. When there is trust and shared decision-making, it is far easier to achieve resilience factor four on the Resilience Factors Table (Table 2.1): challenging how "things have always been done" and being willing to go more deeply into problem-solving and change. When professional development toward change is a natural outcome of collaborations and conversations happening across the school ecosystem, it becomes an effective catalyst. When time for follow-up, synthesizing, and planning is allotted as part of the professional development, teachers can take ownership. It can be discouraging to spend a session learning about something for which no time or space will be designated for unpacking the content, finding its relevance and meaning in the curriculum and to the students, or taking it to the next level. Over time, this pattern can create resistance to the next professional development session. But clinging to "how we have always done it" is a fruitless defense against the unknown (Marzano 2010).

One teacher pointed to her district's work on diversity, equity, inclusion, and belonging. As schools have committed themselves to deepening their understanding of racial, cultural, gender, and learner diversity, equity, and inclusion, they have engaged experts in the field for training and exploration. Critical to the ability of teachers to engage with these ideas; examine their biases, beliefs, and practices; and make sustained change, is the ability to spend time together in hard conversations. New knowledge and skills "need to be backed up with practice," Lisa Mahar insisted.

> Are we meeting the students where they are at? We are looking at every aspect of the child—not just the data, but all the other layers of the child. We need to provide staff with the tools so we can be inclusive....

She further noted that in East Greenbush, much thought has been put into shifting this dynamic.

> This is about scaffolding professional development that is meaningful, and that we build and are intentional about. Principals are supporting the teachers, making sure you

have an hour of release time so that we can get in and do some vetted work and follow up.

That follow-up can take the form of added resources, training, and/or reflection.

Celebrating Growth

As a school honestly reflects on progress, teachers can see where more work is needed and what to celebrate. Spiro Gouras commented on collaboration, growth, and change at Poughkeepsie Day School:

> We are talking all about *processes as we make change together so all team members together* actually know *and feel* what's happening. And then the next thing is celebrating when you've tried something new, done it, and it appears to be working. Feeling like those accomplishments are noted [is key], and there's a whole arc of development in that.

> **Reflect. Act. Learn.**
>
> *When I think about in-service days, people usually come away with either a reaction of 'Wow, we did something new as a group and brainstormed a collective goal that we are ready to move forward on' or 'That was a stupid day.' But along with those kinds of days, there has to be follow-through and time and space for gatherings. When it doesn't happen, teachers become demoralized.*
> – Karen Nichols, teacher-leader

Taking me into the hallway, Spiro pointed to a teacher made chart with all of the community organizations with which Poughkeepsie Day School classes collaborate by grade level, project name, and time of year; an outcome of a collaborative process the faculty went through to tackle a school-wide community service initiative.

Rachel Van Carpels, a middle school language arts teacher at Troy Howard Middle School in Belfast, Maine, affirms this last point: "Celebrating progress is really important. Actually doubling back and saying, 'We've made progress here' gives people the sense that their professional development and collaboration have meant something." When all participants in an organization are swimming in the same direction, that can contribute to and be a reflection of a shared mission and purpose.

In his work with adult learners, Malcolm Knowles developed the six assumptions of the adult learner:

Six Assumptions of Adult Learners

1. Adults have a self-concept
2. Adults have life experience
3. Adults have a readiness to learn
4. Adults have internal motivation
5. Adults are problem-centered
6. Adults have a need to know

We who provide professional development (PD) to teachers ignore these at our peril (Knowles 1979). The feelings teachers describe having after spending time in a professional development session that acknowledge none of these six developmental truths about adult learners are disappointment, skepticism about all professional development, and an increasing resistance to ongoing professional development.

In *The PD Book: 7 Habits that Transform Professional Development*, Elena Aguilar and Lori Cohen write, "*Professional development is defined by its impact. PD is successful if, after the learning experience the learner can do something else, or do something different.*" Knowing what that "else" or "different" is and how that fits into school goals, group goals, subject goals, or individual goals lends meaning and relevance to the learning. Following up on the learning at school signals the importance of the learning (Aguilar and Cohen 2022).

Many of the teachers I interviewed spoke about the experience of "one-off" PD. With all they have to do in the classroom, they only feel it is worth being pulled out of the classroom if the PD is relevant, addresses them respectfully as an adult learner, and gives them something actionable in their classrooms. School leaders need to be clear about what is:

Most Important: What are the priorities for staff development and curriculum development, and who is setting those priorities?

Mandated: How can even mandated PD be made meaningful through debriefings and follow-up?

Most Meaningful: What PD opportunities can target aspects of school culture that are hindering the development of belonging, trust, collaboration, ongoing professional growth, and shared decision-making?

Step 1: Attaining Clarity

Reflect: How can I model remaining open to continuous learning to teachers, staff, and students?	Act: Adopt an instructional leadership role in the ongoing professional growth of teachers and staff.
What does professional learning mean to me?	Identify five of the most meaningful and transformative PDs you ever attended. What made them so?
What are the different kinds, categories, and targets of professional development I would like to do with my staff?	Set priorities, Gather seed group to research options
Is it important to provide individuals opportunities for PD?	Set priorities, survey faculty
How can I use PD to cultivate a resilient teaching community?	Create a flowchart that illustrates where you are, where you want to go, and how PD can catalyze that.

Attaching Growth to Goals

Goals/growing edges	Professional development
School goals Resilient teaching community goals	
Grade level goals	
Subject area goals	
Individual goals	
Performance improvement goals	

Step 2: Assessing Abilities

Reflect: What are the strengths and growing edges of my faculty?	Act: How will I support the learning on the growing edges?
How can I most effectively use observations to assess teachers' strengths and growing edges?	Redesign observation rubrics to be holistic, descriptive, and instructive.
How can I make observations positive and productive, no-fear experiences?	Do away with any vestiges of "gotcha" culture, and build confidence in the observation process.
Does ascertaining professional development goals and activities for the year fall under shared decision-making?	Survey faculty to ascertain interests and goals for PD.
What are my criteria for choosing among PD providers?	Co-create standards for PD that can be used to assess effectiveness.

Step 3: Achieving Completion

The commitment to ongoing learning is never complete. However, arriving at a culture of ongoing learning in which observations, professional development, and follow-up learning are expected aspects of work at school constitutes a form of completion in the context of ongoing learning. What does this look like in your teaching community?

Notes:

7

Engage in Shared Decision-Making

> Getting everyone's opinions and thoughts takes a long time, but then you usually come up with a solution that people can support and that prevents the back-biting that can happen. You need wisdom in the building to help with that.
>
> – Lauren DeGeorgia

Indeed, wise leaders who actively cultivate resilient teaching communities have allowed the teachers participants in this book to effectively engage in their schools' decision-making processes. This dynamic has a direct impact on teaching and learning, the experience kids have at school, and the larger community's feelings about the school.

Literature from the 1960s to the 1990s—beginning with teaching memoirs such as *36 Children*, by Herbert Kohl (1963), and *The Lives of Children*, by George Dennison (1967), and studies such as *The Schools Next Time*, by Donald R. Thomas (1973), among many other examples—documents the changing role of teachers, from obedient conformers in the traditional classroom and school hierarchy to teacher as researcher, instructional designer, activist, and social worker. This evolving notion of "teacher" was honed in academic corners such as Lillian Weber's Workshop Center at City College in Manhattan and continued in earnest into the 1990s with statewide initiatives such as New York State's 1991 New Compact for Learning and the Kentucky Education Reform Act (KERA), which mandated the creation of shared decision-making teams at school and district levels and sought equitable funding and zoning practices to address historic school segregation. These organizations and initiatives viewed teachers as professionals who, because their experience, insights, knowledge, and gathered wisdom deserved a seat at the table when it came to program development, policy-making, and problem-solving.

As in any ecosystem, the roles, cohorts, teams, and departments of a school or district are interdependent. In a healthy ecosystem, interdependence is seen as a strength, and diversity of all kinds, including diverse perspectives, is welcomed. Of course, schools have a hierarchical structure, with each level of the hierarchy dependent on the others and leaders guiding the manner in which the interdependence is understood, expressed, and seen by all cohorts. The more invitational and less hierarchical the systems are the more teachers can contribute and share the load of planning and problem-solving with the leader.

Trusting Teachers, Elevating the Profession

In the years just before the COVID-19 pandemic transformed schools, students, and schooling, some teachers' organizations, study centers, schools, and education programs had begun emerging out of the fog of the standards and high-stakes-testing movement to question and evaluate where they were and wanted to go. In this period, the National Commission on Teaching and America's Future published *What Matters Now: The New Compact for Teaching and Learning*, which looked back over the twenty-five years since the first edition of *The New Compact for Learning* was published and partially implemented in 1991 by Thomas Sobol, New York State's Commissioner of Education. Sobol had the visionary goal of improving education for all students through sweeping changes to everything from funding formulae, to curriculum development and standards, to increasing the role of teachers as "stakeholders" in education. This brought about a wave of shared decision-making and other structural changes to how schools were to run (Cook and Tashlik 2005).

Reflecting on her work with colleagues, Lisa Mahar observed, "It's very important that people feel they have a voice at the table, that they are being heard, and this fosters growth." Will Salley described how Mission Vista High School had done a good job of bringing in all the stakeholders when it started looking for a learning management system. "Instead of it being a top-down, we all came together to look at systems and make a choice. The rest of the staff could say, 'well, I trust these people.'" We talked about how this was not a one-off process in Salley's district. In rewriting their *Portrait of a Mission Vista Student*, teachers, parents, and even elementary students were involved. Will continued, "In deciding on the student pathways course (how students design their educational trajectory at Mission Vista), grading practices, and a statement about AI, shared decision-making was employed." This commitment comes from the superintendent, and the building principal, Jeremy Walden, who carries on the philosophy of shared decision-making at Mission Vista.

But for this level of collaboration to happen, there must be a bedrock belief in the experience, insights, and knowledge that teachers bring to the table, and this is not a belief universally held by all school leaders, all schools, or the education system as a whole—in fact, far from it. In a recent conversation I had with Michael Tempel, longtime educator, and president of the Logo Foundation, he remarked on changing expectations of the teaching profession.

> We have asked all teachers to get master's degrees. They have to take courses along the way, all with the idea of

professionalizing education. But then we give teachers scripted curriculums that are designed to be delivered by teachers with *little pedagogical skill or knowledge of the subject matter*. They are then evaluated based on how their kids do on tests. It's the professionalization of credentialing along with the de-professionalization of teaching practice.

As an example, in 2009, the National Governors' Association and the Council of Chief State School Officers announced the initiative to build the National Common Core State Standards, which were to clarify, unify, and standardize what students learned in all disciplines and grades across the country. "To write the standards, they assembled 'work groups' that included university professors, leaders of education advocacy groups, and experts from testing companies." It was only later, "under pressure from teachers' unions, [that] they added K–12 teachers" (Gewertz 2015).

This pattern of underrating and marginalizing teachers' professional contributions to the development of programs and curricula for which they will ultimately be the conveyance has set up the resistance to change we see among many faculty. This is a natural response that many people have to an asymmetrical relationship between responsibility and authority. Shared decision-making practices allow teachers not only to feel heard but also to lend their expertise, knowledge, and creativity to school-based solutions and endeavors. In fact, an essential component of resilience—the ability to bounce back from setbacks—is the opportunity to be part of the solution. In the resiliency factor table (Chapter 1), our final resilience factor requires teaching communities to "build mechanisms for responding, adjusting, and adapting to real-world change." With the increasing pace and complexity of the issues schools face, leadership cannot manage alone; leaders need to be acting in collaboration with faculty and staff. The school leaders I interviewed have made this connection and committed to it.

Spiro Gouras of Poughkeepsie Day School noted,

> Sometimes it feels very ugly to be micromanaged, but when you tell someone 'let's do this together' and you really mean it; when a request is followed by, 'Would you like to meet about it? Let me know how I can support,' and you actually mean that, people know. They're looking for how what you say is followed up with action.

Rachel Van Carpels talked about leadership styles:

> If you have a concern, and you email or call, and they don't get back to you for days or are placating, that erodes the feeling that they actually want to fix the problem. It is frustrating. On the other hand, the leader who says, 'Who else can we bring into this conversation?' is really involving you, and it communicates they have a real intention to solve the issue.

There is still not sufficient data to *unequivocally* demonstrate that students and instruction in schools with shared decision-making practices benefit from those practices. The website of the UCLA Center for Community Schooling shares a rich trove of history and purpose about community schools. Though the center has committed to shared decision-making to support the ecosystem of organizations that work with the school's population, they address this lack of data about how collaboration, shared decision-making, and ongoing professional development affect school culture, teaching, and learning.

> While much has been written regarding the importance of raising the profile of teachers in school governance and decision-making, the interplay between the formal empowerment of teachers through policy and structural systems and educator decision-making roles in everyday practice is poorly understood.
>
> (Kang et al. 2021)

> **Reflect. Act. Engage in Shared Decision-Making.**
>
> *Getting everyone's opinions and thoughts takes a long time, but then you usually come up with a solution that people can support and that prevents the back-biting that can happen. You need wisdom in the building to help with that. A resilient teaching community is a cohesive group who trust one another and trust decision-making. Any good education system is a two-way street, but you need to recognize shared decision-making because teachers are more willing to try things when they have a seat at the table.*
> *– Lauren DeGeorgia, Teacher-Administrator*

Community Schools continue, as a necessity of their model, to push through barriers to shared decision-making to achieve democratic schools. As a school leader, I was deeply invested in building community, collaboration, and ownership within the faculty. But, taking the time to shape policy and program, make decisions, and solve problems as a teaching community was sometimes trying and contentious work.

Step 1: Attaining Clarity

Many schools, public and independent, have decision-making bodies made up of a variety of stakeholders. The types of decisions made and the process these bodies use is delineated. Does this create a culture of shared decision-making?

Reflect: What are the costs and benefits of being the sole decision-maker?	Act: Analyze categories of decisions I make and determine which categories will benefit from having more people at the table.
Is there a general sense of shared decision-making in my school?	In what cases (types.situations) and ways (informal and formal) do I engage teachers and staff in decision-making?
What are my goals in sharing decision-making?	

What are my resistances?

How will I begin?   What is my action plan?

Attaining Clarity on Shared Decision-Making

Which decisions are open for shared decision-making, which are closed? What are your criteria for each? Are you pushing all the possible doors open? Who are the colleagues that are right for the categories that are open? When and how to schedule shared decision=making is an art and a science that if not done thoughtfully, can undermine trust in the process.

Decision Categories	Open?	Closed?	Who?	When and How Scheduled?

Step 2: Assessing Abilities

Decision-making can take the form of a one-on-one snap decision, a short group process, or a formal curriculum council. For people to trust the decision-making process they need to know that their time and ideas are being seriously considered and their decisions have merit. If the decision-making process adds up to simply getting a pulse on where folks stand, that is not an appropriate use of shared decision-making time.

Reflect: How will I act as arbiter of democratic shared decision-making?	Act: Establish norms for shared decision-making with seed group
How will I engage people in the shared decision-making process?	Create the right opportunities for the right people.
How will I challenge people to step outside of their comfort zones to engage?	Co-create norms with Seed Group for shared decision-making.
What will I model to imbue trust in theprocess?	How will I clarify with each decision-making process, the inherent opportunities and obstacles?
Is it important that I communicate progress?	I will create a collaborative action plan that designates actions, timeline, and people, and make that visible.

Step 3: Achieving Completion

Reflect: What will completion look like?	Act: Write or draw your vision
How will shared decision-making change how we feel and communicate at school?	Create a process for keeping a pulse on how colleagues are feeling, what they are thinking.
How will shared decision-making change my daily work?	Keep a journal tracking the process, what is working, what needs honing.

Is the process inclusive enough? Do I keep going back to the same people?	Cultivate decision-makers. Seek out workshops, PD presenters to continually build skills.
Are the decisions being made solid? Enduring? Practicable?	Co-create rubric for durable decisions. Who and what will the decision affect? Can resources be found to support the decision? Is there consensus?

Part 3
The Working Community

Illustration. The Working Community. Michelle Hughes.

8

Foster a Collaborative Environment

Our division head meets with us every other week, but as a faculty, we decided to meet on the off weeks anyway. When there is trust, and teachers are working in healthy collaboration with each other, there can be a rich exchange of ideas. This leads to teacher-initiated meet-ups at which logistics, curriculum, and students can be discussed, ideas can surface, and solutions can be shared.

– High School Math/Science Teacher

In my conversations with High School English teacher, Jeff Fisher, he shared this insight on the impact of meeting and collaborating on teaching and learning. After meeting,

> we bring a lot more confidence back to difficult situations, which is more important than actually being successful in difficult situations. We're pretty inventive with the things that we do; we are free to decide what are the things we need to and have to do. [After meeting with colleagues] I come back to the classroom fortified psychologically and emotionally for the conversations that the students want to have with me.

Making Time for Collaboration

Teachers readily share the benefits they experience to their well-being, and personal and professional growth, when they engage with, plan with, and problem-solve with colleagues. As concerns about the impact of data-driven standards on teaching and learning were rising in the post-pandemic years, the study by the National Commission on Teaching and America's Future, *What Matters Now: The New Compact for Teaching and Learning*, presented the following vision.

> We have squeezed all we can out of the hard rind of econometric formulas. Now it is time to activate the human factor—the motivation and intelligence of students and educators—to reorganize schools around what drives learning. This will require strengthening relationships among teachers through collaboration, offering opportunities for teacher leadership, and providing supports for teachers to become highly accomplished instructors.
> (National Commission on Teaching and America's Future [NCTAF] 2016)

Teachers are expressing the desire to work with, solve problems with, and create with other teachers to build their teaching practices, support each other, and ward off the negative effects of isolation in trying times. All the teachers with whom I spoke, whether they currently work or have worked within a resilient teaching community, believe collaboration is essential to fostering resilience and a sense of belonging.

The National Education Association (NEA) has shared a video on its website created by the National Labor Management Partnership (2018) that presents "a new model for education partnerships." The partnerships' data show that teacher collaboration yields "greater teacher retention and educator empowerment, more effective communication amongst stakeholders, and most importantly, an increase in student success, even in high-poverty school districts."

Center School middle school English teacher, Mike Veve, provided another example of how collegial sharing enhances his teaching and the student experience. "Whenever we have an idea, we present it to the staff, and you get really great crowdsourced feedback." His colleague Emmy Reiver talked about the importance of this interdependence and connection.

> Our staff meetings—we meet every Tuesday after school—are actually fun; there are a lot of laughs. One thing we do is, if there is a certain student that we are struggling with, if there is a child in my advisory that I'm having a hard time with, we brainstorm about it, so even though this is a child in my advisory, it's everyone's concern. We all feel comfortable sharing. That is what keeps us super resilient.

When school leaders build time for teacher collaborations into the schedule, it sends a message that this practice is valued for the growth it confers upon teachers and for the benefits to teaching and learning. Over the course of writing this book, I had the opportunity to chat with The World of Learning director Pat Mulroy and supervisor Olivia Grugan on their podcast, *We Do This Every Day*. The World of Learning Institute in Altoona, Pennsylvania, provides virtual learning for schools in Pennsylvania that are in need of world language and advanced mathematics teachers. Thus, faculty are from across Pennsylvania and rarely in the same physical space. In discussing how World of Learning cultivates and supports collaborations, Olivia spoke about a planning meeting with four of her faculty. "It was a vibrant meeting. At the end they asked, 'Can we do this again? Can we do it in two weeks?'" Olivia reminded them they could meet on their own. And then she reflected, "If you don't create it intentionally, it will not happen" (Mulroy 2024). Indeed, all the participating schools for this book plan some form of collaboration time, whether professional learning communities, project committees, curriculum councils, or meetings of varying cohorts.

While teacher attrition reached a new peak in 2022, it had already begun to rear its head by 2016. According to data from the 2016 National Commission on Teaching and America's Future, "anywhere from a quarter to half of new teachers [leave] the field in the first four or five years" (NCTAF 2016). Furthermore, fewer people are "lining up to take the place of teachers who leave: enrollments in traditional and alternative preparation and certification routes dropped by 20% in 2013–14 alone" (NCTAF 2016). NCTAF returned to the importance of teacher collaboration and co-mentorship.

> …despite evidence from both international and U.S. studies that show that focused professional collaboration improves teacher retention, satisfaction, and self-efficacy, the majority of teachers never teach together (54%) or even visit each other's classrooms (50%).
>
> (NCTAF 2016)

Teaching is a lonely occupation in some significant ways. The teacher is typically the sole adult in a room with young people for hours, without access to peers. This is compounded by the history of individualism that permeated education for so many years. "I come alive when I close the door to my classroom," or something like it, was a common refrain when I began teaching, and persists among many teachers. However, one of the resiliency factors on the Resiliency Chart is the ability to respond, adjust, and adapt to real-world change. This needs to be an everyone-in-the-pool endeavor. Teachers who participated in the conversations in this book spoke extensively about the importance of collaboration and shared decision-making to their satisfaction and engagement at work; yet, these processes are often overlooked in recommendations for how to retain teachers.

As Karen Nichols of Oakwood Friends observes,

> Space matters in general. *Community* requires the physical connection, the face-to-face, where people can meet and feel heard. Through that regularity of seeing people

in an organic way, you can problem-solve, feel like you are working as a team, and you can get feedback. During the interstices, when people are eating together, intermixing—that's where we have all the meetings that we might never have because 'we don't have the time.' That's when you are laughing and joking. You can say, 'Hey, let me ask you about this kid' or get feedback about something you are doing.

Consistent collaboration and communication allow teams to develop an understanding of each other's styles, talents, and struggles, and they become an operating principle of a school when leadership supports and makes time for them. A RAND report titled "Restoring Teacher and Principal Well-Being Is an Essential Step for Rebuilding Schools" found:

> Many district and school leaders already work hard to build supportive environments and should build on their success. Leaders who have not made adult relationships a priority could consider transferring the strategies they use to build positive student-staff relationships to focus on adults. Leaders might also consider actions that could foster camaraderie among staff—such as intentional opportunities for social interactions—to build positive relationships among different groups of staff.
> (Steiner et al. 2022)

Stephen Haff of Poughkeepsie Day School, agrees.

> I think about faculty meetings vs. professional development. When we teachers have a chance to sit and talk to each other for an extended time about how we are living together here, and how the students we are living with are dealing with what comes up day-to-day, that is super valuable. I've never been in a place where we had that, but here we get to do that twice a week, and we are neighbors. I think that is where development actually happens, with your colleagues.

Manage Conflict

Many of the attributes of resilient teaching communities, and the conditions that foster them, are nurtured through the day-to-day interactions among cohorts and the culture of a school as a whole, and are solidified through structures that bring people together to design curricula, solve problems, and make decisions that affect that culture. Having the patience to work through the collective of faculty and staff, to share and listen to divergent points of view and objectives, and to work through obstacles together, is imperative to arriving at enduring solutions. For the people I interviewed, the patience needed to come to consensus is worth the outcome of working in a resilient teaching community. But close work of this kind can also lead to conflict, as people debate approaches to curricula or problems or dispute policies. In a resilient teaching community, conflict and divergent points of view can broaden perspectives, change minds, and even lead to better solutions.

Jeff Fisher brought it back to the classroom:

> One of the things I've been talking about with the kids recently—during a potentially volatile conversation—was we would find a way through it. And when you can do that, you strengthen all the bonds. Then you are fighting the good fight together.

The third resilience factor from the Resilience Table, calls upon the teaching community to "share and acknowledge hidden beliefs and biases that could get in the way of collaborations and innovations." There has to be a safe space to air these hidden beliefs and biases so they can be resolved. As part of her definition of resilience in a teaching community, Jackie Katzen posited, "The first thing is that there is a respectful environment in which differences can be aired and processed." In fact, several teachers observed that a big part of communication and trust is about managing conflict. Lauren DeGeorgia reflected, "Conflict happens, and that's part of being human, but there is always the bottom line that we are there for each other."

In his book, *The Advantage*, Patrick Lencioni warns that teams that cannot tolerate divergent points of view cannot be healthy (Lencioni 2012). Cultivating healthy conflict is critical to productive teamwork. Yet, in schools, conflict among adults is often seen as a thing to be avoided or shut down. This can have the negative effect of leaving those in disagreement in isolation, where they may feel their only options are back-biting and undermining. Inability to process conflict damages the resilience of the teaching community. In their groundbreaking book *Getting to Yes: Negotiating Agreement Without Giving In*, Roger Fisher and William Ury warn,

> However well you understand the interests of the other side, however ingeniously you invent ways of reconciling interests, however highly you value an ongoing relationship, you will almost always face the harsh reality of interests that conflict. No talk of 'win-win' strategies can conceal that fact.
>
> (Fisher and Ury 2011)

Reivitch's resilience factor five challenges teaching communities to "put challenges/conflicts into perspective, take the big-picture view, identify and focus on the aspirations of the school." Leadership plays a significant role here. Having the long view and mission always in mind, leaders can play a mediating role. When schools establish norms for disagreement and resolution, students and adults grow and expand their points of view and are more willing to express divergent points of view. "We don't always agree," Jeff Simons said, "but we do it with a professional discourse and come to a consensus."

Over the course of twenty years as a school leader, I mediated several conflicts between teachers, and between teachers and managers. Over the course of those years, I found I needed a deeper skill set for this role and began attending mediation workshops at the local mediation center. Later, as the emphasis became restorative practice, I shifted my somewhat ill-informed viewpoints on what this meant and found restorative practice enormously helpful in working with kids and adults.

In my conversations with Maura McNulty and Mary Ellen Tomson, former middle school teachers and deans at the Albany Academies, Maura recalled a situation in which conflict led a leader to bring mediators in: "You can't have mediation without naming the problem, and that is really helpful by itself." Mary Ellen added, "Sometimes people don't have the information they need, whereas Maura's example shows a willingness to disrupt the conflict." To work through a conflict, "There has to be a scrap of trust."

Balance Autonomy and Community

Teachers have to make hundreds of split-second decisions during their teaching and learning hours. Forty years ago, education theorist Madeline Hunter tried to codify these decisions into a framework for excellence in teaching. Her theory was that if she were able to document every decision-making moment in a teacher's day, she could provide teachers with a best-practice solution, thereby increasing the teacher's autonomy and effectiveness.

> My clinical theory of instruction is based on the premise that the teacher is a decision maker. Because no one can tell teachers what to do, my purpose is to tell teachers what to consider before deciding what to do and, as a result, to base their decisions on sound theory rather than folklore and fantasy.
>
> (Hunter 1985)

While there were many merits to Dr. Hunter's research, there were considerable flaws: (1) no one can possibly identify and codify all the decisions a teacher makes in a day; (2) Hunter's premise is based on the notion that left to their own devices, teachers will make decisions based on "folklore and fantasy" rather than experience, background knowledge of their students, a cultural understanding of their school and school community, and myriad other variables Hunter could not have anticipated. The education machine did with Hunter's model what it does with many teaching and learning models—it turned it into a means for assessing teachers.

However, Hunter's revelation and focus on the fact that teachers are decision-makers was promising. Knowing teachers are making hundreds of decisions in a day could lead schools to examine the kinds of decisions teachers are making in the classroom, the kinds of decisions they are making in teams, and the scope of school-based and district-based shared decision-making teams. This kind of collective analysis could inform what autonomy looks like. In 1998, Dr. William Glasser wrote *The Quality School*, in which he laid out the premise of his "choice theory": "Humans and other mammals are driven to do all they can to **Survive**." Once survival is reasonably secure, he continues, our four essential needs are love, belonging, freedom, and fun. Our freedom "to move, think, and express ourselves freely" motivates us "to learn new, useful behaviors" (Glasser 2007).

Glasser then merged his theory with the work of industrialists Joseph Juran and W. Edward Deming, namely their model of total quality management, which gives each worker responsibility and authority over the work they do, whether in a car manufacturing plant or a watchmaking studio. According to Glasser's choice theory, with each mandate, curriculum change, and standard that teachers have had little to no opportunity to shape, while bearing all the responsibility to enact, there is a corrosion in their sense of self-efficacy and well-being (Glasser 1998).

Some organizations and corporations, including start-ups, have carried forward the work of balancing accountability with authority in a current model known as RACI (Responsible, Accountable, Consulted, and Informed), which charts the roles of people working on a project or in a team. The goal is to balance these four roles within a group to maximize both autonomy and communication (Miranda and Watts 2022). Deming and Glasser paved the way for the RACI model, and school leaders seeking to build resilient working groups might consider how elements of this model could be adapted and adopted to assist them in finding the balance between autonomy and community.

For example, in the East Greenbush Central School District in New York, teachers have broad participation in curriculum councils and policy committees and also feel free to make decisions in their classrooms, or turn to each other for mentorship or brainstorming when needed. East Greenbush teacher Maegan Asenbauer reflects, "While we have a consistent curriculum, there are so many facets we can work with. We have the ability to be autonomous."

In teaching, there is a natural tension between autonomy and community. Most teachers I have worked with and known crave creative and academic freedom. Given the opportunity, they will develop curricula that incorporate their own interests and passions with those of their students. As Center School director Elaine Schwartz noted, "People have to be able to try things. That is ownership." However, autonomy can also lead teachers back to their silos, which can defeat other critical attributes of resilient teaching communities: collaboration, shared decision-making, and belonging. Autonomous silos can also lead to a disjointed educational journey for the student, one that lacks cohesion and a continuum of learning.

Principal Crystal Thorpe, advocated for teacher-created programs that enriched the school while providing the opportunity for teachers to collaborate and co-create based on the notion that autonomy balanced with community led teachers to feel more engaged with their work, while in Vista, California the district is working with a curriculum construct first developed by Robert Marzano and Richard DuFour in 2001, the "guaranteed and viable curriculum." This model embeds teacher collaboration in curriculum development, calling upon teachers' experience and understanding of what is essential in the standards and what lessons and classroom experiences work best to teach it, and then incorporates the input of students in how they will be assessed (Marzano et al. 2001).

Vista is doing this work alongside developing equitable grading practices. Michelle Daum, English department chair and teacher, recounted her one-on-one conversations with colleagues about how they were feeling about this work.

> Such an important part of who we are is the community we have here. So we were asking them, 'What has supported you on this journey to engage in the work?' They all said they felt they had permission and safety to take risks. 'We are all expected to engage [in the curriculum process] to some extent, but I have freedom to decide to what extent I am going to engage in this work ... and to decide how.' That shared decision-making is there as well, and it's always focused on valuing teacher time and making the work meaningful to us as a staff.

Teachers need "autonomy, flexibility, and efficacy to make the determinations they need to in the classroom, within the framework of the structures of the district," said Superintendent Jeff Simons.

> "So it's autonomy and flexibility, and being able to participate in the greater good of the organization. And we hope the teachers feel, 'We see that the central leadership and board understand that our primary role is to educate the kids, and there's a framework put in place for curriculum development and planning that is coherent.' When people feel they are working in a framework that makes sense, they feel safe investing in that."

Reflect. Act. Collaborate.

Collaboration ...it's being able to decide which person has the most advanced skill in the area that I specifically need the support in, and knowing that I would always make time to be available to anyone else.
  – Jackie Katzen, veteran elementary educator and professor, SUNY Ulster, Stone Ridge, NY

Step 1: Attaining Clarity

A collaborative environment builds connection, efficacy, and continuity, reduces isolation, and builds consistency across curriculum and the qualities of interactions within and across cohorts.

Reflect: What does true collaboration mean to me? What goals and values are embedded in my idea of collaboration?	Act: Brainstorm a list or create a visual depicting what collaboration looks like.
What personal qualities, strengths, and experience do I bring to collaborations with colleagues?	What is my role in collaborations with teachers and staff?
What is the role of mission and group goals in collaboration?	How do I express how collaboration fits into the larger mission and goals of the school?
What opportunities for collaboration currently exist for teachers and staff? How are these working?	Create an action list that highlights effectiveness and addresses challenges.
What collaborative opportunities am I able to create?	How can I innovate on the current ways meetings happen?
Am I clear on when to collaborate and when to be a sole decision-maker? What is in my way?	Analyze the strategic goals for the year, the current projects and tasks, or daily questions lend themselves to a collaborative process?
Obstacles to Collaboration?	How can I surmount them?

Step 2: Assessing Ability

In every group, there are the talkers, the observers, the facilitators, the critics, the idea people, and the doers. Using each person's strength, while seeking to make each group productive, takes knowing who plays which role and how to optimize their strengths.

Reflect: What strengths and abilities make a good collaborator?	Act: How will I cultivate these strengths and abilities in my community?
Have I talked less and observed enough to know what group role each teacher and staff member takes?	Create an inventory of collaborative strengths
Which teachers find time to collaborate with each other on their own?	Who will comprise my seed group?
Which teachers use collaboration regularly in their classrooms?	How do I improve capacity and interest in collaborative learning?
In collaborations, conflict can occur. How do I tolerate conflict?	Conflict can be healthy. What norms and approaches will I establish for managing conflict?

Sample Inventory of Collaborative Strengths using Habits of Mind

Listens with empathy and understanding	Thinks Interdependently	Communicates with Clarity and Precision	Creates and Innovates	Asks questions, poses problems	Strives for Accuracy	Remains Open to Ongoing Learning	Find Humor and Responds with Wonderment and Awe
Joe						Joe	Joe
	Casey		Casey			Casey	

Step 3: Achieving Completion

What will it look like when you have cultivated a culture of collaboration?

Reflect:	*Act*
Have I been as consistent a collaborator as I can be?	What is in my way? How do I surmount this?
Have I pulled all the levers to create time for collaboration? Am I supporting those who collaborate on their own?	How do I use schedule, meeting configurations, and subs to make space for collaboration?
Is collaboration integrated into the student experience?	Have I provided PD opportunities for teachers to develop collaborative learning experiences for their students?
How is the school culture changing among faculty and staff?	I will assess changes through…

9

Focus on Mission and Vision

> I think that one of the things that took it out of me during the pandemic was that the mission suddenly became not as clear. When we came back, everyone had such different needs, and there was a vacuum of leadership. To feel a sense of collective resilience, I need to be in a situation where the values are aligned and intellectual growth is paramount.
> – Maura McNulty, Middle School English and Dean

I worked for some years under a head of school who, in his yearly school opening addresses, would post visuals of fish swimming in the same and opposite directions from each other. His message: swim together in the same direction, and our work, our school, and the student experience will be more satisfying, cohesive, and culture building. I agreed but felt that a common vision of what we were swimming toward was missing. Having a shared mission and purpose allows a group of people to be focused and productive because they are generally swimming in the same direction. For the schools and educators in this book, a common mission, the *why*, is critical to their sense of purpose and community.

Whether a school is public or independent, democratic processes that are part of the mission, which begins at the top, trickle down into the classroom, where children are called upon to make choices and solve problems together. The impacts of a shared mission cannot be overstated.

School Models and Missions

I've always thought it fortunate for students and teachers that there are so many school models: public, independent, and parochial, magnet and charter, prep, progressive, Montessori, or Steiner. Some have strong and enduring missions and philosophies that draw teachers and students who subscribe to them, and this can naturally lead to the cultivation of a resilient teaching community.

In cities such as Los Angeles, New York, and Chicago schools of choice exist in both public and independent realms. The Center School, for example, is just one of hundreds of schools of choice in New York City. Each of those schools of choice carry their own mission, focus or theme, and pedagogical approach. As a resident of the Mid-Hudson Valley, I lament the fact that our students and teachers lack those free alternatives that allow one to land in the kind of school meant for them. However, there are school districts such as East Greenbush, New York or Montecito, California, where the commitment to seeing and inviting all members, and ensuring that students and teachers thrive, opens the doors to success for a diversity of teachers and learners.

Resilience and a Shared Mission: Independent Schools

As someone who served on the New York State Association of Independent Schools Accreditation Commission, I had the opportunity to visit and read about many independent schools across the northeast. Independent schools' mission statements have both historical and pedagogical dimensions. How, when, and by whom the school was founded forms the firmament of the mission, even as the objectives and means for achieving them change. It is the mission of the independent school that normally attracts a teacher to a particular school. Independent schools tend to be mission-focused.

Many established independent schools maintain the attributes of resilient teaching communities as a tradition, holding these practices among the tenets of a mission that dictates that the school operate democratically and rely on shared decision-making in its regular operations.

For many of the teachers in this study, the common passion and love for teaching is a mission that connects them to one another. One teacher described this as support and professionalism, seeing that the teachers, staff, and everyone else at the school have the best interests of the students at heart. Mary Ellen Tomson, looking back at her time as a middle school history teacher, recalled:

> I always had a mentor, someone I could trust and who would teach me and lead me. But also, there would be enough of us moving in the same direction, led by the same values, that we could keep moving ahead, past the chaos.

As you have read, the teachers of Poughkeepsie Day School, a ninety-year-old progressive independent school in Poughkeepsie, New York, have thrown themselves into the work of recovering their school from the financial fallout of the pandemic because of their commitment to the history and mission of their school. Through the uncertainty of their school's future and an uphill battle for enrollment in a time of declining student populations, they proceed each day with optimism and a commitment to the pedagogical philosophy of their school.

It is often in the face of adversity, that teaching communities redefine, or reconnect to mission. Education consultant Elaine

Chu reflected on the importance of a community foundation of shared mission, values, and resilience:

> First, you have to like kids. There has to be unity around that, which brings integrity, coming back to core values, not letting go of what is true. Then, facing adversity is not just plowing through. It's when we had opportunities to talk about who we were that helped us to come back to being unified in our core identity.

Maura McNulty, a former teacher at the Albany Academies, shared a different experience: In my travels to the midwest for this book, I had the opportunity to meet with a very new teacher, Sam Plauche, who is teaching humanities at Fusion Academy in Chicago. The school's mission—"Guided by a fundamental belief in the immense potential within every person, our mission is to help each student flourish—emotionally, socially, and academically—through positive, mentoring relationships and a personalized education experience"— is translated through a three-word guiding practice, "love, motivate, teach." Sam's feeling is that the teachers at Fusion are drawn there by the mission, the one-on-one teaching practice, and the innovative environment, which stretches from the teaching and learning model to how teachers are compensated.

"I'm definitely there because of the mission and how it plays out," Sam confirmed.

> There are a lot of opportunities to collaborate, even though we work with individual kids. Actually, recently the science teacher and I realized that with science papers, the students can do the science with him and the writing with me.

Sam went on to describe the leadership as supportive and trusting of the teachers, who, in turn, are inclusive and affirming in their work with each other.

Resilience and a Shared Mission: Public Schools

Public schools have the broad mission to educate the populace. Individual districts will have mission statements or mottoes, which can be shaped by faculty, staff, and board and/or by forces such as state initiatives and movements in public education. For many public school teachers, it is the broad mission of providing a public education that draws them. For some, it is the sense of connection to a particular community or school.

Heidi Van Nes, a retired English as a second language teacher, spent time in many classrooms, got to know many families, and worked tirelessly for thirty years to maintain the connection between her students and their school. In her letter to me, Heidi wrote,

> The involvement of the entire community is essential to succeeding, and cohorts must cooperate and work as closely as possible to keep parents, principals, teachers, and students engaged and committed to long-term goals in curriculum and community participation. Smaller schools in real neighborhoods are indisputably more effective at getting the community to care about what happens in school, and the selection of the people and leaders designated to make this happen.

Within the public school system in many cities and municipalities, alternative models such as the small schools movement, schools of choice, and magnet schools have come to prominence. Their missions may be theme-based, focused on the sciences, arts, or leadership, or pedagogically driven, adhering to progressive or Montessori approaches, for example.

Community Schools of choice are founded by groups of educators, parents, nonprofits, colleges, and service organizations, extending collaboration beyond the school walls to community partnerships. The network of community schools now stretches across the country providing wraparound services for students and families at school.

The importance of community involvement was never more apparent than during the COVID-19 pandemic shutdown and disruption. In reflecting on this, East Greenbush superintendent Jeff Simons said,

> Our teaching staff feels they are part of the community, so when an emergency such as the pandemic required them to shift to distance learning, something they were never prepared to do, [because of] their sense of pride in the district, their investment in the community, and their care for the students, they did awesome things that really surprised me.

In facing the pandemic, teachers' connections to teaching, students, their colleagues, and their mission allowed some schools to maintain a certain momentum in teaching and learning, while the absence of these attributes led others to falter and even fail. Mike Veve described what happened at the Center School during the pandemic:

> Anecdotally speaking, our kids—emotionally, socially, academically—were in a much better place [than those at other schools]. Even in remote and hybrid learning, we were able to maintain trust, ties, and communication at a level that is higher than at some other schools.

A Common Framework

When schools adopt a common framework for thinking and communicating, this can catalyze and focus leaders, teachers, and students' thinking and communicating. One example is the Habits of Mind framework. The Montecito and Vista, California school districts have become certified Habits of Mind Learning Communities of Excellence, as a framework for academic and community growth. It also connects them to a community of schools that have all adopted the Habits of Mind to support their missions and the objectives they set for teaching and learning.

Resilient Teaching Communities in Two International Habits of Mind Learning Communities of Excellence

The Habits of Mind are sixteen unique thinking strategies and dispositions identified and organized into a framework by education theorists, Bena Kallick and Art Costa. The Institute for Habits of Mind was founded by Kallick and Costa to support schools in bringing the Habits of Mind into the academic and cultural lives of schools, through training, staff development, and school certification. To learn more about the Habits of Mind visit www.habitsofmindinstitute.org

Montecito Union Free School: I met Rusty Ito at the Institute for Habits of Mind conference in Vista, California. I was there to participate and present, and I was looking forward to talking with educators from schools that are certified in Habits of Mind. I also wondered what role the Habits of Mind goal of "making the world a more thoughtful place" might play in the development of these resilient teaching communities.

Montecito Union Elementary is the single school of the Montecito School District. In my conversations with Rusty Ito, I asked about how he builds trust and supports the ways that collaboration and shared decision-making happen. As assistant principal, Rusty focuses on being visible, accessible, and engaged. "I'm rarely found in my office," he noted.

We followed up on our conversation at the conference by phone, and we were able to focus on the role leaders play—and more specifically, the role Rusty plays—in cultivating a resilient teaching community. "I see my role largely as relationship building. Whether it is with students, faculty, or staff, I take the time to have real conversations." This approach to administration, coupled with the ability to get things done, is what builds trust and allows the forward momentum in schools like Montecito.

I asked about the role that Habits of Mind plays in the focus on collaboration and shared decision-making at Montecito. "It's really in everything, isn't it?" he responded. That, indeed, was the message of the conference. The Habits of Mind are not a unit of study or discrete curriculum. They are meant to be integrated and applied as any habit would be in the teaching, learning, and relating within a community.

Mission Vista: I also had the pleasure of meeting and having follow-up Zoom calls with Will Smalley, photography teacher, and Michelle Daum, English chair, at Mission Vista High School.

Mission Vista is a magnet high school in the Vista Unified School District with a concentration on the arts. Over lunch at the Habits of Mind conference, both Michelle and Will talked about the bonds formed among faculty through their shared mission.

Will talked about the balance of autonomy and community that the faculty had during the pandemic:

> Those are the things that allowed us to thrive and continue to do the work we want to do. During the pandemic, I had to redo everything—we were given the autonomy to do what we needed to do to support our kids. It was challenging and inspiring. We spent a lot of time boiling the standards down to what our essential standards are—what are the things we really need to teach. That work has continued—we've been working with the guaranteed and viable curriculum.

Michelle observed,

> The Habits of Mind for us is about helping students to be successful in all levels of the classroom. Whether

it's in the striving for accuracy within content or collaboration they are using. Whether it's classroom content goals, or the overarching goals that we are working towards as a faculty in developing our students, these are the dispositions they need to be successful.

> **Reflect. Act. Align.**
>
> Not all schools have the option to write a mission statement, others evaluate and revise their mission every few years. Whether yours is a school within a large district with an overarching mission, or a Montessori or Waldorf School in which the model and mission are historical, or a school with an individual mission, there is value in having periodic discussions about the mission, how the school aligns with the mission, and what the common drives and vision are for the professional community that are not expressed in the mission.

The *Why*

The articulation of mission and vision among faculty, staff, students, and families bolsters the sense of belonging to their schools, not simply teaching or learning there. Meagan Asenbauer shared, "Good teachers remember the *why*—why we chose to dedicate everything to kids." Her colleague Lisa Mahar added, "When you have passion, you are going to come to work every day, and when you feel supported and respected, you are going to stick with it."

When the Mission Is Historically or Institutionally Established

Leader's Reflection

Here is an example of a district-wide mission statement and school-based review. On the empty chart below, use your school district or historical mission to reflect.

It is the mission of the — District to nurture the intellectual curiosity, knowledge, skills, and social awareness students will need to meet the responsibilities and advantages of our diverse and dynamic society.

Keywords	A Strength in our school: How So?	A Growing Edge for our school: How so?	What other Keywords pertain to our school?
Nurture	We provide free meals, are always in touch with families to support, and attend to students' special needs	Our low test scores have put pressure on teachers and students to move quickly through curriculum, sideline creativity, and limit student movement	Community-based Commitment Low-retention
Intellectual curiosity		We struggle to provide opportunities for students and teachers to inquire and experiment	Young teachers Teacher-to-teacher Mentorship
Knowledge	Vibrant commitment to literature	Content knowledge is limited by skills teaching Teaching out of discipline area Need for professional learning	**What Drives Us?** Care for our community
Skills	We have increased reading and math skills, and have engaged families in their development	Have more to go to meet standards	Serving a vulnerable population Love of teaching
Social awareness	Traditions to celebrate all cultures, school-wide voting, growth mindset	Need to find acceptable path toward social emotional literacy	Love of children Love of my discipline
Meet Responsibilities	etc.	etc.	etc.
Advantages diverse			
Dynamic			

OR

Waldorf education's mission is to develop the whole child, and to help students become independent thinkers and lifelong learners			
Keywords	A Strength in our school: How So?	A Growing Edge for our school: How so?	What other Keywords pertain to our school? What Drives Us?

Leader's Action

1. Lead sessions at small group meetings (admin, grade levels, disciplines, etc.) in which participants work together to fill the chart out.

   - Is there alignment among the charts?
   - What are the common understandings and threads?
   - In which areas are we meeting the mission?
   - How do our keywords and drives mesh with this mission? Which stand out as unique for our school?

2. Once all groups have met, ask for a volunteer from each group to form a task force that will create a school-based vision statement that …

   - incorporates the unique aspects of the school
   - complements the overarching mission
   - reflects the drives of the professional community

   An example might look like this:

   At the Lawrence School we are committed to increasing opportunities for students and teachers to question, inquire, and create as they endeavor to build knowledge and increase skills. We are driven to create a school in which families participate, basic human needs are met, and students thrive and learn to their greatest capacity.

3. Have the writers present a draft of the vision statement to their cohort, and ask for feedback. Once the statement has been tweaked by the writers, share with the faculty.

When the Mission Statement Is School-Based

Schools with individual missions are typically guided to review and revise the mission every five years. This review is an opportunity to analyze…

- Whether what the mission says is a reflection of what is really happening
- Whether the mission needs to expand to incorporate new initiatives, tenets, or philosophical underpinnings
- Whether there are anachronisms that need to be reevaluated
- Whether the mission captures the aspects of the school that are distinct, palpable, and enduring

  1. The leader would benefit from doing the analysis as a Reflection before meeting with professional cohorts and board of trustees.
  2. When professional cohorts have completed their charts, craft a draft of the revised mission with a representative group.
  3. If appropriate to your school: Present the draft to your Board of Trustees for final contributions and a vote.

Overarching Mission Review and Vision Statement

District or Association Mission Here			
Keywords	A Strength in our school: How So?	A Growing Edge for our school: How so?	What other Keywords pertain to our school? What Drives Us?

Vision Statement:

Individual School Mission Reflection

Your Mission Here			
Keywords	A Strength in our school: How So?	A Growing Edge for our school: How so?	What's New? What's Anachronistic?

Part 4

Obstacles, Impacts, and Reflections

Illustration. Obstacles, Impacts, and Reflections. Michelle Hughes.

NOTES

10
Obstacles to Resilient Teaching Communities

There are many obstacles to the cultivation of resilient teaching communities. Union contracts and the narrow definition of the teacher's work, grueling schedules that do not make time for collaborative processes, regressive policies, and leadership that is distrusting of the empowerment of teachers are all examples of the obstacles that leaders and their teams must face. In this chapter, we first explore four broad categories of obstacles to resilient teaching communities: the culture wars, the effects of standards and high stakes testing movements of the 21st century, turnover rates of school and district leaders, and the historical definition of teaching.

The Culture Wars

In a time of deep division and parent activism, culture wars could understandably be an obstacle to school leaders establishing shared decision-making teams for school and district leaders. These forces, combined with school violence and shootings, have led some schools, school leaders, teachers, and staff to feel under siege, which can lead some institutions to close ranks. When these conditions diminish the sense of community within a school, there are real obstacles to teaching community resilience. In his NEA Today's article, "The Culture War's Impact on Public Schools," reporter Tim Walker interviewed Professor John Rogers, at the Graduate School of Education and Information Studies at UCLA and the director of UCLA's Institute for Democracy, Education, and Access. In his research, Rogers surveyed public school principals, and found almost half (45%) of principals said the amount of community level conflict—centered largely around opposition to inclusive curricula—during the 2021-22 school year was "more" or "much more" than prior to the pandemic.

Walker goes on to affirm the importance of the attributes of resilient teaching communities, collaborative support, professional development, and constructive engagement in collectively facing the assaults of the culture wars. "When leadership is not being supportive, nor providing real professional development, it sends a signal to teachers—and has a chilling effect on this very important work" (Walker 2023).

However, schools that can create avenues for communication, collaboration, and belonging within the school community and face these challenges together, means no one professional is facing these forces alone. Yet, public school districts and some independent schools have historically tended to not do a particularly good job of engaging parents and other community members in a constructive and inclusive way. Due to this history of resisting meaningful engagement with parents and community, the skills and dispositions needed to manage this crisis have, on the whole, not been cultivated and practiced.

One example of a curriculum that has recently come under fire in the culture wars are social emotional learning (SEL) programs. Without clarity and communication within a school community about the purposes and means for teaching social literacies, concerns arise about intrusiveness, purposes, and the tax on academic learning that might be taking place. This can lead to conflicts between schools and their communities, and as a result schools might capitulate to forces they can't manage. An example of this capitulation comes from my region, in which a school district suspended a consultant's social emotional literacy work with students and staff due to the complaints of one very influential parent. Working together as a teaching community to clarify and communicate priorities, mission, purposes and means of teaching and learning are critical in a time when the vigilance of parents and communities is at a peak, and a bulwark against the fear-based decision-making that the school district felt backed into. This preemptive collaborative and communicative approach shores up the support for teachers who can be on the front line of attacks.

Leadership Turnover

While the general sense is that Superintendent turnover is high, in fact it is not universally so. The likelihood that a superintendent will leave a district after three years increases with the size and urbanity of the district. In his rural and relatively small centralized district, East Greenbush superintendent, Jeff Simons could well get his wish and fall into the category of superintendents who stay with a district for years (Grissom, Jason A. and Stephanie Andersen 2023). One could draw the corollary that if principal effectiveness has the kind of impact on school culture, achievement, teachers, and students, then certainly superintendents have this impact on principals. High turnover of superintendents impacts principal performance, and has strong ripple effects down the chain of command. In a 2022 Harvard Edcast conversation among superintendents, Carl Cohn said this about the superintendency.

> …in a time where there seems to be a lack of moral leadership, people are often looking to their local leaders, people like school district superintendents for the kind of honest and moral leadership that we need today. We tend to want to trust our local leaders. So the job is just absolutely crucial to not only the health of our communities, but I think the health of our democracy.

We have established the importance of school leaders to the academic and cultural flourishing of a school. When transitions are frequent, sustaining trust, belonging, collaborative practices, and relevant and supported professional development become challenging. A three-year turnover rate of superintendents, and four-year turnover rate of principals and teachers in many districts, particularly those in most need, undermines every aspect of resilient teaching communities.

Both the Center School and Poughkeepsie Day School were undergoing leadership change during the course of my writing this book in 2023. When I visited these schools, neither John Reilly, the new principal of Center School, nor Spiro Gouras, the new Head of School at Poughkeepsie Day School, could be found in his office. John was sitting on a bench in the hall, talking and reviewing materials with a teacher and greeting students. Spiro was walking with a teacher, returning from a visit to a classroom. In my conversations with them, they evinced genuine curiosity about the work teachers were doing with students. Both enjoy brainstorming and planning and allow these interactions to influence their leadership and goals. These are leaders who are seeking to both honor and further the strengths and achievements of their schools while exploring areas for growth. But not all transitions are so smooth.

Richard DuFour, in *The Principal as Staff Developer* (1991), emphasizes that the leader's role in shaping missions and vision necessitates a collaborative process with the teaching corps: "In order for a vision to guide and motivate the people within an organization, it must grow out of their needs, hopes, and dreams." To realize this, the leader must take the time to learn and value what the faculty's needs, hopes, and dreams *are*. John O'Reilly and Spiro Gouras are taking that time, feeding the resilience of the teaching community, and building trust as a result. The short terms of leaders in many schools hobble the ability for deep change to occur over time, and cultivating resilient teaching communities in many cases requires deep change (Levin and Bradley 2019).

The Age of Standards and High-Stakes Testing

As a supervising teacher and school leader, I readily passed on the adage to student teachers and faculty, *teach the kids in front of you*, handed down to me from my mentors. This means putting aside our agendas and expectations and really seeing and responding to the students in the classroom. This has never been more important than now, when kids are in a different place academically, socially, and emotionally from where they would be expected to be due to the impacts of the COVID-19 pandemic. And with strict standards in place around the country, it has never been more difficult to do so as a teacher.

At the turn of the 21st Century, all indicators were pointing to a more innovative, learner-centered revolution in learning. Models for 21st Century Learning abounded, such as the Framework for 21st Century Learning set forth by the Partnership for 21st Century Learning. However, the standards and high stakes testing movement happened instead. By the time the first round of the standards movement as outlined by the national *No Child Left Behind* legislation fully matured in 2001, teachers' evaluations had begun to become formulaic. By the time, National Common Core Standards were in place, these evaluation practices had become quantitative, tied to students' performance on tests.

When students and teachers began breaking down under the pressure of the testing, the outcry was immense. I was a public school teacher at the time in an inclusive setting, which meant that a significant number of my students had learning and/or emotional disabilities. Teachers in my team were asking,

> What can test scores possibly tell you about how we work with students, how we plan projects or set up classrooms for engagement and growth, or how early we arrive in the morning and how late we leave in the evening to fulfill our mission as educators?

What was startling was how disempowered our school leaders were, offering few avenues for managing the radical changes required under these new mandates.

In *How Leadership Influences Student Learning*, a 2004 research review, Kenneth Leithwood, Karen Seashore Louis, Stephen Anderson, and Kyla Wahlstrom observe,

> ...organizational conditions sometimes blunt or wear down educators' good intentions and actually prevent the use of effective practices. In some contexts, for example, high-stakes testing has encouraged a drill-and-practice form of instruction among teachers who are perfectly capable of developing deep understanding on the part of their students. And extrinsic financial incentives for achieving school performance targets, under some conditions, can erode teachers' intrinsic commitments to the welfare of their students.
>
> (Leithwood et al. 2004)

In the two decades since the onset of standards and testing-based education, we haven't traveled as far as we might have expected on the journey to school improvement. The standards and high-stakes-testing movements and their attendant teacher-evaluation systems have, in fact, adversely affected the hallmarks of resilient teaching communities. In 2000, just before the adoption of No Child Left Behind led to widespread high-stakes testing, Mary Alice Barksdale-Ladd and Karen F. Thomas conducted an investigation in two states on the impact of standardized-testing regimens and found:

> In the call for accountability, teacher decision making about what is best for children and notions of developmentally appropriate instruction appears to have been dismissed. Teachers are being asked to behave as received knowers rather than constructed knowers, and in turn the expectation is that children will be received rather than constructed knowers. Although teacher education programs have worked hard to create programs

that prepare constructivist teachers, public schools have apparently turned away from this understanding of teaching and learning.

The standards and high-stakes testing movements have diminished teachers' sense of efficacy and decision-making ability in their classrooms. In many schools, scripted curriculum negates the need for curriculum design, collaboration, or shared decision-making. Shared decision-making practices vary from state to state, and within states, from district to district. The fealty and consistency with which district and school leaders implement shared decision-making will affect how the participants value it. As one parent described her experience on her district shared decision-making committee, "The superintendent makes decisions and then shares them with us," leaving this community member feeling deflated by the experience, rather than connected and invested.

Education theorists and writers, Yong Zhao and Jim Watterston, saw the pandemic as an opportunity to hit the reset button on education broadly and the work of teachers specifically. In their article "The Changes We Need: Education Post COVID-19," they write,

> With ubiquitous access to online resources and experts… the role of the teacher changes. … Instead, the teacher serves other more important roles such as organizer of learning, curator of learning resources, counselor to students, community organizer, motivator and project managers of students' learning. … Teacher education needs to focus more on preparing teachers to be human educators who care more about the individual students and serve as consultants and resource curators instead of teaching machines.
>
> (Zhao and Watterston 2021)

However, as much as the realities they describe are true, scripted curricula, standardized testing, and top-down decision-making persist. And when innovative changes to teachers' work are instituted in schools, these changes can quickly be subject to evaluation—one way we kill initiative and creativity in education.

The Changing Role of Teacher

Historically and currently, the role of teacher is defined by teacher-student contact time, which generally delineates the teacher's work and workday. These are the times teachers are engaged in teaching, advising, or other supervisory duties. Thus, several of the activities delineated by the seven attributes can be seen as being extra, or in public schools, in contravention with the work rules in a contract. The resistance to rethinking the roles and responsibilities of teachers is hardwired into the psyche of education. The role of the teacher in the resilient teaching community begins with being a committed and passionate educator of students *and* reaches beyond that role to include research and development, collaboration and co-creation, problem-solving and decision-making, as well as being a cultural steward and a mentor. This teacher has grown her leadership and negotiation skills and is conscious of the big picture—the school beyond her classroom door.

Instituting this expanded role elevates the teaching profession and diffuses the feeling of powerlessness that teachers often feel and cite as a reason for leaving the profession. Participating at this level also changes the teacher day, the duties enumerated in contracts, and *should* ultimately affect pay. Though these adjustments are challenging, the schools in this book find creative solutions around meeting and committee structure due to the desire that teachers have to connect and collaborate. The leaders' ingenuity in cultivating the seven attributes of resilient teaching communities allows for this expansion of professional engagement to flourish. One teacher described "the magic" of the school being in the acceptance and support teachers feel and their ability to innovate. However, in her school's 2023 union-district negotiations, the teachers' collaborative time was sacrificed. Leadership of the school is finding creative ways to preserve the myriad collaborations the school had cultivated because the teachers had become invested in their work with colleagues, and they are hoping collaboration will come back in future negotiations.

Schools that are committed to cultivating resilient teaching communities find creative ways to advance the activities that help them flourish without flouting contracts. For example, instead of whole faculty meetings, some principals are breaking the faculty into small group meetings where curriculum and co-planning can be done, and they are designing schedules so that team members have breaks at the same time. Making the expanded role of teacher à la carte, in which teachers adopt roles they are naturally drawn to and good at, allows for a differentiated experience for the adults and capitalizes on professional capacities.

"Old models of leadership are not doing it anymore," Ross Hogan observes.

> Educators, staff, they won't stand for it; it does not work in our culture anymore. Resiliency has a lot to do with morale. The degree to which teachers are excited and looking forward to coming in the next day and teaching depends on the degree to which their voice is being heard and they have agency in their teaching.

Dana Goldstein, author of *The Teacher Wars: A History of the Most Embattled Profession*, knows a thing or two about old models. In an interview about her book she describes one of the most important early founders of public education, Catherine Beecher, who in the 1820s entreated women to teach because they are uniquely suited to do so: "Mothers lead children in the home, and teachers lead children in the classroom." Beecher assured young municipalities that these women would do it for 50% less pay than men. This, Goldstein asserts, set in motion the "cheapness" factor that still plays into every level of decision-making about school funding. While early teachers had a great deal of autonomy in the classroom itself, they had little personal autonomy in the outside world, setting the template for a woman's profession that continues to be restrictive, poorly compensated, and hierarchical (Goldstein 2013). Today, eight out of ten teachers are women, while only one in four superintendents in public education are women (Phillips 2023).

In her 2023 study of women heads of independent schools, "Networking and Adapting Their Way Forward: Women Heads of Large, K–12 Independent Schools and Their Leadership Literacies," Jessica R. Flaxman writes,

> Since 2009, the number of women leading all independent schools has increased from 31% to 41% in 2021. ... Although gender bias is a known and acknowledged factor in this disproportionality, incomplete stories persist about what holds women back. Questions about, and analyses of gender disparity in leadership continue to place the locus of control and blame on individual women rather than the broader system that consistently recognizes, rewards, promotes, and maintains male leaders across all sectors and organizations both national and globally.
>
> (Flaxman 2023)

The role of teachers is, in part, mired in this history and reinforced through a lagging representation of women in leadership. But it is also stubbornly intransigent because the wheels of change in large systems turn so slowly.

11

Impacts of Resilient Teaching Communities

In this chapter, we focus on two broad areas of school life that resilient teaching communities impact. In Kids, Teaching, and Learning we explore how cohesive and accepting teaching environments lead to healthier learning environments, and more robust curriculum continuity. In longevity and continuity, we'll show how these healthier learning environments lead to teachers and leaders staying and the impacts of that longevity.

Kids, Teaching, and Learning

"We show kids that if we can be ourselves, so can you. These kids are so special, are so unapologetic and unafraid to be who they are. We foster a community where people are unafraid to be themselves," Middle school teacher, Emily Reiver, shared as she reflected on the impact her teaching community has on kids.

Of the 168 hours in a week, we are generally awake for 105 of them. Kids and teachers spend roughly 40 of those 105 hours together. Almost half of our kids' waking hours are spent at school. What happens when they do not feel they belong? What happens when the educational setting is fraught, chaotic, or rigid, and what happens in the classroom when the teacher is isolated and/or demoralized? In her letter, Veteran ENL teacher Heidi Van Nes wrote, "Resilience and tenacity make all the difference; students who are genuinely interested and respected as thinkers and individuals will thrive. Those who feel ignored and alienated will burn out."

Superintendent Jeff Simons has witnessed the impact of the sense of belonging among children at the East Greenbush Central School District. "Overwhelmingly, kids like coming to school here," he told me.

> They take their cues from the teachers, who are overwhelmingly happy to be at work and show this. So when a kid comes to school, is greeted by a happy English teacher with a warm classroom environment, who makes [the kids] feel special, they say, 'I'm in.' The teachers send positive messages, and that is infectious.

One teacher I interviewed, whose faculty meets twice a week, said, "This kind of consistent collaboration is bound to have an enormous impact on the level of innovation." And this positively affects the classroom and student experience.

Mission Vista High School is taking a multi-pronged approach to supporting their students. They have worked collectively and carefully on Robert Marzano's guaranteed and viable curriculum model, in which teachers and administrators examine the standards to discern what is "essential" and what is actually doable and co-create a curriculum map that allows for individual style but ensures a continuum of learning. Streamlining the curriculum in this way, the students are supported to go more deeply. Teacher Michelle Daum describes the role of leadership in the network of student support.

> They know every kid—their name, face, and every single story. Our leadership meets with students at risk every week.... They've said, before you get started on content, build relationships, take that time, build that connection. Make sure you know every kid—their name, their face, their story.

Wallace Foundation researchers looking into how leadership influences student learning asked and explored "…who or what educational leaders should pay the most attention to within their organizations.?"

> Teachers are key, of course, and impressive evidence suggests that their "pedagogical content knowledge" (knowledge about how to teach particular subject matter content) is central to their effectiveness. So, too, is the professional community teachers often form with colleagues inside and outside their own schools….
>
> …At the school level, evidence is quite strong in identifying, for example, school mission and goals, culture, teachers' participation in decision making, and relationships with parents and the wider community as potentially powerful determinants of student learning. District conditions that are known to influence student learning include, for example, district culture, the provision of professional development opportunities for teachers aligned with school and district priorities and policies governing the leadership succession. Districts also contribute to student learning by ensuring alignment among goals, programs, policies and professional development.
>
> (Leithwood et al. 2004)

As leadership sets the tone for positive risk-taking in teachers, a teacher sets the tone for positive risk-taking in their students. In such teaching and learning communities, as students see teachers willing to practice the habit of mind, *taking responsible risks*, to create and innovate, they are more likely to do so as well. In my observations of teachers over my years as a school leader, when teachers engaged students in discovery, opened multiple entry points to learning and showing understanding, and created an environment of curiosity, students were more willing to venture, to take risks themselves. The participating teachers in this book consistently share positive examples of how their own sense of creative license in the classroom impacts student learning. Moreover, in collaborative schools that cultivate a sense of belonging, students themselves can become co-constructors of school culture. Mission Vista photography teacher Will Salley talked about rebuilding school culture post-pandemic with students who had not been in a brick-and-mortar school for almost two years. "With the seniors being the only students here on campus who had been here for two years, we told them, 'We need you to be the leaders. How do we build that culture back in?'"

The Community Schools Network took a twenty-year look back at its work in their 2019 paper "Twenty Years, Ten Lessons." In their exhaustive review, authors Jane Quinn and Martin Blank found positive corollaries between collaboration, teacher retention, and student and community well-being. One of the markers of community well-being in schools is attendance.

> We have seen that when educators work together with families and community partners, by using the community school strategy, they can make significant inroads in reducing chronic absence and addressing its underlying causes. For example, New York City Department of Education data released during the Fall of 2019 indicates that over the five-year period covering the academic years 2013–14 through 2018–19, New York City community schools decreased chronic absenteeism by 9.6%, nearly 20 times the citywide decrease of 0.5%.
>
> (Quinn and Blank 2019)

A 2024 *New York Times* article found that,

> nationally, an estimated 26 percent of public school students were considered chronically absent last school year, up from 15 percent before the pandemic, according to the most recent data, from 40 states and Washington, D.C., compiled by the conservative-leaning American Enterprise Institute.
>
> (Mervosh and Paris 2024)

When students enjoy and want to go to school, attendance increases, and that in itself has major impacts on learning. Attendance has been a project in many of the schools I visited and for school leaders I spoke with. "Our truancy rate was at 20 percent% last year," assistant principal Rusty Ito shared, "We worked with families and put our attention to all the aspects of truancy. This year we are at 6 percent."

> Students in a school with a principal who is above average in effects on attendance (i.e., at the 75th percentile) go to school approximately 1.4 days more in the typical school year than do students whose principal is below average (i.e., at the 25th percentile).14 Students are also 4 percentage points less likely to be chronically absent (i.e., to miss more than 10 percent of the school year) in a school with an above-average principal.
>
> (Grissom et al. 2021)

When school communities are able to coalesce around significant issues like attendance, they can make an impact. A positive and welcoming school climate confers a wide range of benefits on student experience, teaching, and learning. But just as important is a school's ability to take positive and thoughtful action to respond to challenges, to harness the power of *real-time resilience.*

> Because real-time resilience is about challenging your beliefs and putting things into perspective, the more you practice those skills, the better you will become at this one. Real- time resilience is used the moment that the adversity first strikes — that is why it is such a powerful tool.
>
> (Reivich and Shatté 2002)

David Levine, founder-/director of the Teaching Empathy Institute reflected "It goes beyond participating in school-based committees"; they feel what Levine calls "certainty." He explained: "Certainty of their place and their role leads to their full participation in the life of the school.... When teachers feel that certainty, they can create it for their students." In fact, there is a growing body of research exploring this connection, and this is driving the development of union initiatives that are making cultivating resilient teaching communities more possible.

The United Federation of Teachers (the New York City arm of the American Federation of Teachers) has been working with the city's Department of Education on the Progressive Redesign Opportunity Schools for Excellence (PROSE) initiative, "a program predicated on the UFT's core belief that schools work best when all members of the community feel respected and the word 'collaboration' is not just a cliché" (United Federation of Teachers). Schools that apply and are accepted into the PROSE initiative have demonstrated their ability to collaborate around the development of innovative programs and curricula, and are supported to broaden and deepen those practices. Though elements of progressive redesign of schools have been in place around the country since the 1970s, this union initiative marks a turning point in the union's perspective on the teacher's role, reflecting its acceptance of the premise that when teachers are collaborating, problem-solving, and decision-making, teachers and students benefit.

East Greenbush Response to Intervention coordinator Lisa Mahar observed that an environment that supports innovation has this positive outcome: "Kids are saying, 'I feel like I can be myself, I can take risks,' and this lets them be their best selves." Her colleague Meagan Asenbauer agreed: "Kids are willing to put forth effort and recognize the teachers as allies. We have a community that trusts what is happening in the classrooms. For some kids, the school building is the safest place they will be."

High school English teacher, Jeff Fisher, observed, "When kids see teachers and school leaders engaging with each other as people, they see a model for how to engage with each other as well." Citing a particularly dicey sensitive conversation in class, he noted, "One student was afraid of being embarrassed, but that never happened." It is this sense of belonging Fisher has instituted among his students helps them build the resilience to work through challenges. Mike Veve of the Center School connects the dots between teacher and student resilience: "Resilient teaching is about learning how to manage chaos, disruptions, changes in plan. Resilient teachers model resilience for the kids."

Continuity and Longevity

One of the common threads related to continuity and longevity that participating schools shared was the number of teachers who had been students in the school. Kitti O'Neill, school counselor at Fishers Junior High School, shared, "I think I am a good example of this. I went to school here, and when as an adult I saw there was an opening, I was so excited. Just the fact that so many teachers were still here fifteen years later says a lot." While retention is not the same as resilience, everyone I interviewed felt the two are interconnected—that teachers are more likely to continue teaching in an environment that is highly collaborative and in which they feel a true sense of belonging. "Everyone in this building really cares about each other, cares about doing a good job and making it a great experience for the kids." Kitti added.

When asked about how she carries on the missions and traditions of the Center School, director Elaine Schwartz said, "As new teachers come into the school, they are taught by the faculty, traditions, philosophy, the ways we do things." Teachers want and need mentorship and collaboration of this kind, and when they receive it, resilient teaching communities are fostered in turn. Center School alumnus and teacher, Jake Walkup, recounted, "We have a high number of students who come back to visit as well; they keep us up with what they are doing, and families keep in touch long after their kids have graduated," and how many returned to teach. "I knew since I was an eighth grader at the Center School that I wanted to come back to teach," Emmy said. "It's a place like no other."

Teachers cited the importance of teacher leaders, particularly those who mentored and modeled best practices for them in teaching, collaboration, and teamwork. Some teachers described this as wisdom, others as mentorship. What seems clear is that, in the best of circumstances, veteran educators hold and pass on the values, traditions, and rules of thumb needed for new teachers to succeed and grow.

Elaine Schwartz emphasized the importance of "having people to look up to, having a thread and a history, and a feeling that they are still present in the work and celebrated in many different ways." She added, "[This] needs to come through the leadership and mission, the day-to-day, and into student work. It has to be visible." While most leaders will not have the lengthy tenure Elaine Schwartz did, longevity is critical to school development and continuity. Principal Crystal Thorpe was adamant on this point: "It takes five years for any meaningful change to take hold. When people leave leadership after four years, there can't be any forward movement. Put that in your book."

My time at Fishers Junior High School abounded with teacher accounts of admiration for their principal, Crystal Thorpe. "I wouldn't work for another principal" or "She always supports us," were common refrains and spoke to the positive climate of this junior high school. This comports with evidence from Tennessee surveys that teachers in schools with principals who receive higher supervisor practice ratings report more positive climates. Relatedly, studies have found that in schools where principals are given high overall average ratings from their teachers, teachers report higher job satisfaction. They also are less likely to report an intent to leave the school or to turn over in that school year (Grissom et al. 2021).

Fishers Junior High School, Fishers, Indiana: A Day with Crystal Thorpe

I drove through miles of cornfields from Chicago to Fishers, Indiana, in the shadows of a multitude of wind turbines, to arrive at Fishers Junior High School. I found Crystal meeting with her assistant principal Tige Butts, (who is now Principal of Fishers, as Crystal has moved up the ranks of leadership) Sharing their experience working at Fishers with me, I learned that Crystal has been at the school for sixteen years, and Tige for twelve. I would learn throughout the day that people stay at Fishers, citing the sense of community, dedication to kids and excellence, and an appreciation for the kind of leadership that Crystal and Tige offer.

In fact, I was drawn here by an article that appeared in *Education Week* after the acute phase of the pandemic. Principal Crystal Thorpe had written about how, at a time when school leaders were asking their faculties to do more, she was asking hers to do less. I thought, "I've got to talk to this woman!"

It was at the very start of this project on resilient teaching communities, and I was talking to as wide a sampling of teachers as I could find about what this term meant to them. After speaking with Crystal, I became bound and determined to get to Fishers to see her school for myself. Throughout my day, I visited with Crystal and with teachers—both individuals and teams—to test out what have become the seven attributes of resilient teaching communities.

Demographically, Fishers stands out from the rest of the district as most diverse in several ways. The student body is 25% minority, and 12% of students receive free or reduced-cost lunch. The free lunch breakdown defies stereotypes: one hundred of the receiving students are white, and just twenty-five are African American (the remainder belong to other minority groups). Though the school may not have the highest scores in the district it has made the most yearly gains for the past three years.

Walking around the school, the sense of place and the feeling of belonging expressed by adults is mirrored in the students. It was palpable.

The longevity of leaders is essential to the resilience and continuity of a teaching community and has impacts on teaching and learning (Levin and Bradley 2019). Reflecting on his career as a district leader at two different districts, and understanding the importance of continuity and longevity of leadership, Jeff Simons says, "I want to be able to say I was the longest-serving superintendent of two districts, I think there is a lot of research that shows stable superintendent leadership is a major factor in student achievement and school culture." Albany Academies dean Lauren DeGeorgia observed that continuity and longevity result in "strong wisdom in the building, teachers who have been there, with strong beliefs and direction," which then brings new teachers into the culture and philosophy of the team and school. When there is a core of teachers who have internalized school history and culture, they can become an inestimable resource for novice teachers. The willingness to engage with and support next-generation teachers is critical but not assumed. That too has to be written into school culture and expectations. The resilient teaching *community* embodies the notion that while some teachers and leaders may come and go over time, the school community retains continuity through a core of educators that carry on the mission and traditions of the school and pass them on to new members, thereby sustaining the resilience of the teaching community.

> **Reflect. Act. Focus on Mission and Vision**
>
> **SWOT Analysis:** Obstacles to and Impacts of Resilient Teaching Communities

A SWOT analysis is a method for analyzing the path toward change. It asks the participants to list Strengths, Weaknesses, within the school community and Opportunities and Threats from outside the school community. Typically, it is done in this format. I give examples of items a faculty might include.

Strengths:	Weaknesses:
Individual talents and know-how	Historical baggage: distrust, mistreatment, favoritism?
Group strengths, talents, and know-how	Resources: time, training, funds, direction?
Community support	Lack of leadership or community support.
Leadership is on Board	Undermining behaviors

Opportunities:	Threats:
Professional Development and Learning: organizational, leadership, educational consultants	Budgetary Constraints
	Union Constraints
	Lack of community support
Institutional Longevity, Continuity, Consistency	Lack of leadership continuity
School-wide Well-being	
Growing Teaching and Learning expertise	

Parking Lot: When the SWOT analysis is ready to be finalized, process the items that were tabled for later and placed in the parking lot. Some questions you might ask are:
How do we feel about these items now? Should they be included now, and why? Shall we keep them in the parking lot and revisit them later? Or shall they be omitted?

SWOT Process

Step 1: Small groups develop SWOT analyses. Instructions are to add everything.

Step 2: Groups come together for a whole group process. Large Blank SWOT analysis chart is posted.

- Scribes from each group add their data
- Facilitator leads a consensus vote to determine which items remain which are combined, and which go in the parking lot. Facilitator teaches consensus voting as follows: When I call out an item raise

  - Four fingers—if you strongly support
  - Three fingers—if you support
  - Two fingers—if you are neutral
  - One finger—if you strongly disagree

- Any item with strongly disagrees votes is off the table
- Any item with one strongly disagrees vote is in the parking lot until the end of the process

When the SWOT is complete leaders might ask the group to reflect. A handout with the following questions and your commitments at the bottom will provide a structure. Decide whether these will be collected, if so, whether folks need to identify themselves:

1. Do we have the strengths and opportunities to develop and sustain our resilient teaching community? Which are most significant for you?
2. Do you feel clear about what the personal give and get of this endeavor are?
3. In what ways will this endeavor toward collective resilience will positively impact our…
4. School culture?
5. Student learning?
6. Here are my commitments as your school leader:

This data is meant to help you and the faculty actively pull from Strengths and Opportunities, and plan for how you all will manage Weaknesses and Threats. These are follow-up conversations to be had in smaller divisional and department meetings.

Final Thoughts

When Teachers Stay: Cultivating Resilient Teaching Communities aims to offer teachers and leaders a map of sorts leading toward culture change and collective resilience, with the voices of some courageous educators to reinforce that it is all possible. A leader and faculty committed to being a resilient teaching community will work together to maintain the seven attributes that represent the findings of this book and the foundation of their teaching community's resilience. As the leader and faculty develop and incorporate processes to cultivate community resilience, and as the teachers' workday and responsibilities expand, they will need to take creative approaches to making sustainable choices regarding budget, time, and local union negotiations. The strategies suggested by studies and utilized by participating schools in this book are there to learn from, adapt, and adopt. Shifting the job description of teachers to co-creators and teacher-leaders requires collaborative and supportive leadership and trust. As teachers and leaders find their way into their expanded roles, we step away from what we have known for the 200 years of compulsory education, as one of the founders of American public education, Catherine Beecher, envisioned it, and elevate the profession of teaching.

Acknowledgments

I must begin with thanking my first reader, Amy K. Hughes, Ed., for her invaluable guidance, encouragement, and editing prowess in the creation of this book. Amy, you are my superhero! Thank you to my husband and champion, John, for doing everything else while I squirreled away in the attic, writing, writing, writing. To my daughters, Sahana and Eliza, for their unflagging encouragement. To family and friends, thank you for your belief in this project, love, and support. Heartfelt gratitude to Bena Kallick, Doris Gonzalez Easton, and Jacqueline Katzen for loaning me some of your precious summer reading time to be critical friends. Your feedback made this a better book. To Heidi Hayes Jacobs, a million thanks could not fully capture the feeling I have for your support and for your incisive and beautiful foreword.

The powerful ideas in this book come directly from the educators who answered my surveys and wrote or spent time with me, generously sharing their experiences and reflections. It was an extraordinary experience, and I am so grateful to the following schools and educators for their participation:

Participating Schools: Though I did not yet have a full understanding of what a resilient teaching community was at the beginning of this research, I chose these five sites for this research because they seemed to exhibit qualities that indicated resilience and community. These schools are varied by the age group they serve; their urban, suburban, and rural demographics; their public or independent school status, and their missions.

The Center School, New York, New York: Founded over forty years ago, The Center School is a survivor of the small public progressive schools movement in New York City and serves over 200 middle school students.

Poughkeepsie Day School, Poughkeepsie, New York: An independent school in Poughkeepsie, New York, which, with the help of faculty, staff, and parents, is working hard to recover from a closing in 2020. PDS serves students from pre-kindergarten through twelfth grade.

East Greenbush, New York, School District: Located in upstate New York, East Greenbush School District is noted as a great place to work. Superintendent Jeff Simons and I met to talk about why. I had conversations with three teachers from the district to get their points of view as well.

Fishers Junior High School: Located in Fishers, Indiana, and led by Crystal Thorpe, Fishers Junior High School is a vibrant and innovative public school where teachers and students feel connected and engaged.

Mission Vista High School located in Vista, California, is an arts-focused public high school in the Vista School District that has integrated many of the attributes of resilient teaching communities. Vista has committed itself to the adoption of Kallick and Costa's Habits of Mind framework.

Voices: Participants in this research were either from the school sites chosen for the research, or were educators who are currently working in environments that exhibited some of the qualities of a resilient teaching community, or had done so in the past. They are varied in their roles, grades, subjects, and areas, as well as schools in which they teach.

Meagan Asenbauer, high school English teacher, Columbia High School, East Greenbush Central School District, East Greenbush, New York

Elaine Chu, veteran elementary school teacher and founder, Institute for Imaginative Inquiry, New York, New York

Michelle Daum, teacher and English department chair, Vista, California

Lauren DeGeorgia, middle school world language teacher and dean, The Albany Academies, Albany, New York

Tania de Rosier, elementary and middle school world language teacher, Albany, New York

Doris Easton, veteran teacher and former associate head of school, High Meadow School, Stone Ridge, New York

Jeff Fisher, high school English teacher, Poughkeepsie Day School, Poughkeepsie, New York

Joy Frush, middle grades English, Fishers Junior High School, Fishers, Indiana

Olivia Grugan, Supervisor, World of Learning Institute, Altoona, Pennsylvania

Stephen Haff, multi-disciplinary teacher, Poughkeepsie Day School, Poughkeepsie, New York

Ross Hogan, principal, Duzine Elementary School, New Paltz, New York

Rusty Ito, Assistant Principal, Montecito Union School District, Montecito, California

Jackie Katzen, veteran elementary school teacher and professor, SUNY Ulster, Stone Ridge, New York

David Levine, Director, Teaching Empathy Institute, Stone Ridge New York

Lisa Mahar, Response to Intervention coordinator, East Greenbush Central School District, East Greenbush, New York

Maura McNulty, former middle school English teacher, The Albany Academies, Albany, New York

Pat Mulroy, director, World of Learning Institute, Altoona, Pennsylvania

Karen Nichols, high school humanities teacher, math and science chair, professional development coordinator, Oakwood Friends School, Poughkeepsie, New York

Sam Plauche, humanities teacher, Fusion Academy, Chicago, Illinois.

Jenna Pyle, middle grades social studies, Fishers Junior High School, Fishers, Indiana

Emmy Reiver, middle school multi-disciplinary teacher, The Center School, New York, New York

Esther Rosenfeld, former principal, Central Park East II, and director of Principal's Institute, Bank Street College of Education, New York, New York

Will Salley, photography teacher, Mission Vista High School, Vista, California

Elaine Schwartz (Now deceased), director, The Center School, New York, New York

Jeff Simons, superintendent, East Greenbush Central School District, East Greenbush, New York

Kelyn Snyder, middle school social studies teacher, Goff Middle School, East Greenbush Central School District, East Greenbush, New York

Shira Teich, high school math-science teacher, Poughkeepsie Day School, Poughkeepsie, New York

Crystal Thorpe, Former principal, Fishers Junior High School, Fishers, Indiana

Mary Ellen Tomson, former middle school history teacher, The Albany Academies, Albany, New York

Rachel Van Carpels, middle school language arts teacher, Troy Howard Middle School, Belfast, Maine

Heidi Van Nes, retired English as a second language teacher, Highland Central School District, Highland, New York

Mike Veve, middle school English language arts and special education teacher, The Center School, New York, New York

Jake Walkup, middle school multi-disciplinary teacher, The Center School, New York, New York

Sources

Aguilar, Elena. 2018. *The Onward Workbook: Daily Activities to Cultivate Your Emotional Resilience and Thrive*. San Francisco, CA: Jossey-Bass.

Aguilar, Elena, and Lori Cohen. 2022. *The PD Book: 7 Habits That Transform Professional Development*. San Francisco, CA: Jossey-Bass.

Barksdale-Ladd, Mary Alice, and Karen F. Thomas. 2000. "What's at Stake in High Stakes Testing: Teachers and Parents Speak Out." *Journal of Teacher Education* 51, no. 5, 385.

Barnum, Matt. 2023. "Teacher Turnover Hits New Highs across the U.S." *Chalkbeat*, March 6. https://www.chalkbeat.org/2023/3/6/23624340/teacher-turnover-leaving-the-profession-quitting-higher-rate

Biron, Bethany. 2023. "Employees Are Checked Out at Work More Than Ever—And It Doesn't Matter It They're Remote, Hybrid, or Onsite, Gallup Study Finds." *Business Insider*, January 25. https://www.businessinsider.com/employees-checked-out-work-more-than-ever-gallup-study-2023-1#:~:text=A%20new%20Gallup%20poll%20found,remote%2C%20hybrid%2C%20and%20onsite

Brown, Brene. 2012. *Daring Greatly: How the Courage to Be Vulnerable Transforms the Way We Live, Love, Parent, and Lead*. New York: Avery.

Cook, Ann, and Phyllis Tashlik. 2005. "Making the Pendulum Swing: Challenging Bad Education Policy in New York State." *Horace* 21, no. 4. https://essentialschools.org/horace-issues/making-the-pendulum-swing-challenging-bad-education-policy-in-new-york-state/

Covey, Stephen M.R. 2018. *The Speed of Trust: The One Thing That Changes Everything*. New York: Simon and Schuster.

DuFour, Richard. 1991. *The Principal as Staff Developer*. Bloomington, IN: National Educational Service.

Fisher, Roger, and William Ury. 2011. *Getting to Yes: Negotiating Agreement Without Giving In*. New York: Penguin Books.

Flaxman, Jessica R. 2023. "Networking and Adapting Their Way Forward: Women Heads of Large, K-12 Independent Schools and Their Leadership Literacies." *Frontiers in Education.* https://www.frontiersin.org/articles/10.3389/feduc.2023.1086688/full#:~:text=Since%202009%2C%20the%20number%20of,%25%20to%2041%25%20in%202021

Franco, Marguerite, and Susan Kemper Patrick. 2023. "State Teacher Shortages: Teaching Positions Left Vacant or Filled by Teachers Without Full Certification." *Learning Policy Institute*, July 27, 2023. https://learningpolicyinstitute.org/product/state-teacher-shortages-vacancy-resource-tool

Gewertz, Catherine. 2015. "The Common Core Explained." *Education Week*, September 30, 2015. https://www.edweek.org/teaching-learning/the-common-core-explained/2015/09

Glasser, William. 1998. *The Quality School.* New York: Harper-Perennial.

Glasser, William. 2007. "The Glasser Quality School." *Journal of Adventist Education*, February/March 2007. https://circle.adventistlearningcommunity.com/files/jae/en/jae200769030406.pdf

Goldstein, Dana. 2013. *The Teacher Wars: A History of America's Most Embattled Profession.* Visalia, CA: New America Foundation.

Grissom, Jason A., Anna J. Egalite, and Constance A. Lindsay. 2021. "How Principals Affect Students and Schools: A Systematic Synthesis of Two Decades of Research." Wallace Foundation. https://wallacefoundation.org/sites/default/files/2023-09/How-Principals-Affect-Students-and-Schools.pdf

Hanover Research. 2019. "Infographic: Tackle the Top Drivers of Teacher Attrition." https://www.hanoverresearch.com/reports-and-briefs/tackle-the-top-drivers-of-teacher-attrition/?org

Harter, Jim. 2023. "U.S. Employee Engagement Needs a Rebound in 2023." *Gallup Workplace,* January 25. https://www.gallup.com/workplace/468233/employee-engagement-needs-rebound-2023.aspx

Hive Networks. 2022. "What Is a Working Community?" https://www.hivenetworks.com/workingcommunities

Hunter, Madeline. 1985. "What's Wrong with Madeline Hunter?" *ASCD*, February, 1985. https://files.ascd.org/staticfiles/ascd/pdf/journals/ed_lead/el_198502_hunter.pdf

Kang, Rebekah, Marisa Saunders, and Kyle Weinberg. 2021. "Collaborative Leadership as the Cornerstone of Community Schools: Policy, Structures, and Practice." *UCLA Center for Community Schooling*, March 1. https://communityschooling.gseis.ucla.edu/collaborative-leadership/

Knowles, Malcolm. 1979. "Where Does Training Fit into the Adult Education Field?" *Training and Development Journal* 33, no. 12. https://eric.ed.gov/?id=EJ220639

Leithwood, Kenneth, Karen Seashore Louis, Stephen Anderson, and Kyla Wahlstrom. 2004. *How Leadership Influences Student Learning*. Learning from Leadership Project: Review of Research. Wallace Foundation. https://wallacefoundation.org/sites/default/files/2023-07/How-Leadership-Influences-Student-Learning.pdf

Lencioni, Patrick. 2012. *The Advantage: Why Organizational Health Trumps Everything Else in Business.* San Francisco, CA: Jossey-Bass.

Levin, Stephanie, and Kathryn Bradley. 2019. "Understanding and Addressing Principal Turnover: A Review of the Research." National Association of Secondary School Principals and Learning Policy Institute. https://learningpolicyinstitute.org/sites/default/files/product-files/NASSP_LPI_Principal_Turnover_Research_Review_REPORT.pdf

Levine, David. 2020. *Field Guide to School of Belonging*. Stone Ridge, NY: Teaching Empathy Institute.

Lin, Luona, Juliana Menasce Horowitz, Kiley Hurstand, and Dana Braga. 2024. *Race and LGBTQ Issues in K-12 Schools: What Teachers, Teens and the U.S. Public Say about Current Curriculum Debates*. Washington, DC: Pew Research Center. https://www.pewresearch.org/social-trends/2024/02/22/race-and-lgbtq-issues-in-k-12-schools/

Marzano, Robert. March 4, 2010. "Dr. Marzano on Second Order Change." Marzano Research, Solution Tree: Dr. Marzano on Second-Order Change. [Videofile] https://duckduckgo.com/?q=solution+tree+marzano+on+second+order+change&ia=videos&iax=videos&iai=https%3A%2F%2Fwww.youtube.com%2Fwatch%3Fv%3DtqRWXv6ZTLk

Marzano, Robert, Debra Pickering, and Jane Pollack. 2001. *Classroom Instruction that Works*. Alexandria, VA: Association for Supervision and Curriculum Development.

Marzano, Robert, Timothy Waters, and Brian A. McNulty. 2005. *School Leadership That Works: From Research to Results.* Alexandria, VA: Association for Supervision and Curriculum Development.

Mervosh, Sarah, and Francesca Paris. 2024. "Why School Absences Have 'Exploded' Almost Everywhere." *New York Times*, March 29, 2024.

Miranda, Dana, and Rob Watts, "What Is A RACI Chart? How This Project Management Tool Can Boost Your Productivity". *Forbes Advisor.* Updated: Dec 14, 2022, 2:20pm.

Mulroy, Patricia. 2024. "Building Resilient Communities." *We do this every day…* [Podcast]. World of Learning Institute. https://patmulroy.substack.com/p/building-resilientcommunities

National Commission on Teaching and America's Future. 2016. "What Matters Now: A New Compact for Teaching and Learning." https://files.eric.ed.gov/fulltext/ED572432.pdf

National Labor Management Partnership. 2018. "Collaborating for Student Success." YouTube Video, Posted by National Education Association, November 19, 2018. https://www.youtube.com/watch?v=J-TtmF9q8oM&t=148s

Nguyen, Tuan D., et al. 2022. "Teacher Shortages in the United States." *Teacher Shortages*.org. https://www.teachershortages.com. Accessed November 12, 2022.

Phillips, Vicki. 2023. "Women in School District Leadership: Rarer Than You Think." *Forbes.* https://www.forbes.com/sites/vickiphillips/2023/03/17/women-in-school-district-leadership-rarer-than-you-think/?sh=62d3a7613879

Psynet Group. 2024. "The Order of Change." https://psynetgroup.com/the-order-of-change/

Quinn, Jane, and Martin, J. Blank (The Metropolitan Center for Research on Equity and the Transformation of Schools). 2019. "Twenty Years, Ten Lessons: Community Schools as an Equitable School Improvement Strategy." *VUE* 49, no. 2. https://steinhardt.nyu.edu/sites/default/files/2020-10/Twenty%20Years%2C%20Ten%20Lessons.pdf

RAND Corporation, 2021. "Community Resilience." https://www.rand.org/well-being/community-health-and-environmental-policy/portfolios/climate/focus-areas/community-resilience.html

Reeves, Douglas. 2006. *The Learning Leader*. Alexandria, VA: Association for Supervision and Curriculum Development.

Reivich, Karen, and Andrew Shatté. 2002. *The Resilience Factor: 7 Keys to Finding Your Inner Strength and Overcoming Life's Hurdles*. New York: Three Rivers Press.

Rizvic, Sejla. 2023. "Teachers, Facing Increasing Levels of Stress, Are Burned Out." *New York Times*, March 13. https://www.nytimes.com/2023/03/13/education/teachers-quitting-burnout.html

Rowe, Margaret Anne. 2021. "NAIS Research: Insights into Head of School Turnover." *National Association of Independent Schools*, March 30. https://www.nais.org/learn/independent-ideas/march-2021/nais-research-insights-into-head-of-school-turnover/

Senge, Peter, ed. 2000. *Schools That Learn: A Fifth Discipline Fieldbook for Educators, Parents, and Everyone Who Cares about Education*. New York: Doubleday.

Sinek, Simon. n.d. "Start with Why: How Great Leaders Inspire Action." *Ted Talk*. https://www.ted.com/talks/simon_sinek_how_great_leaders_inspire_action/transcript?referrer=playlist-the_10_most_popular_tedx_talks

"Sobol v. Sobol." 2007. TC People, Teacher's College, Columbia University. https://www.tc.columbia.edu/articles/2007/october/sobol-v-sobol/

Steiner, Elizabeth D., Sy Doan, Ashley Woo, Allyson D. Gittens, Rebecca Ann Lawrence, Lisa Berdie, Rebecca L. Wolfe, Lucas Greer, and Heather L. Schwartz. 2022. "Restoring Teacher and Principal Well-Being Is an Essential Step for Rebuilding Schools: Findings from the State of the American Teacher and State of the American Principal Surveys." *RAND Corporation*. https://www.rand.org/pubs/research_reports/RRA1108-4.html

Strozzi-Heckler, Richard. 2007. *The Leadership Dojo: Build Your Foundation as an Exemplary Leader*. Berkeley, CA: Frog Books.

Thomas, Donald L. 1973. *The Schools Next Time: Explorations in Educational Sociology*. New York: McGraw Hill.

Thorpe, Crystal. 2022. "Why One Principal Is Asking Her Staff to Do Less: How to Get Back to the Basics." *Education Week*, November 1. https://www.edweek.org/leadership/opinion-we-are-going-toslow-everything-down-why-one-principal-is-asking-her-staff-to-do-less/2022/11

United Federation of Teachers. n.d. PROSE (Progressive Redesign Opportunity Schools for Excellence). https://www.uft.org/your-union/uft-programs/prose

Walker, Tim. 2023. "The Culture War's Impact on Public Schools." *NEA Today National Education Association Magazine,* February 17. https://www.nea.org/nea-today/all-news-articles/culture-wars-impact-public-schools

Zhao, Yong, and Jim Watterston. 2021. "The Changes We Need: Education Post COVID-19." *Journal of Educational Change. Educ Change* 22, 3–12. https://doi.org/10.1007/s10833-021-09417-3

Further Reading and Materials

Aguilar, Elena. 2018. *The Onward Workbook: Daily Activities to Cultivate Your Emotional Resilience and Thrive.* San Francisco, CA: Jossey-Bass.

Glasser, William. 1998. *The Quality School.* New York: Harper-Perennial

Goldstein, Dana. 2013. *The Teacher Wars: A History of America's Most Embattled Profession.* New York: Doubleday

Hanover Research. 2019, "Infographic: Tackle the Top Drivers of Teacher Attrition." https://www.hanoverresearch.com/reports-and-briefs/tackle-the-top-drivers-of-teacher-attrition/?org

Harter, Jim. 2023. "U.S. Employee Engagement Needs a Rebound in 2023." *Gallup Workplace,* January 25. https://www.gallup.com/workplace/468233/employee-engagement-needs-rebound-2023.aspx

Marzano, Robert. 2024. "Guaranteed and Viable Curriculum." *Marzano Research.* https://www.marzanoresources.com/professional-development/guaranteed-and-viable-curriculum#conIframewrapp

Reeves, Douglas 2006. *The Learning Leader.* Alexandria, VA: Association for Supervision and Curriculum Development.

Rowe, Margaret Anne. 2021. "NAIS Research: Insights into Head of School Turnover." *National Association of Independent Schools,* March 30. https://www.nais.org/learn/independent-ideas/march-2021/nais-research-insights-into-head-of-school-turnover/

Senge, Peter, ed. 2000. *Schools That Learn: A Fifth Discipline Fieldbook for Educators, Parents, and Everyone Who Cares about Education.* New York: Doubleday.

Sinek, Simon. 2009. "Start with Why: How Great Leaders Inspire Action." *Ted Talk.* https://www.ted.com/talks/simon_sinek_how_great_leaders_inspire_action/transcript?referrer=playlist-the_10_most_popular_tedx_talks

For Product Safety Concerns and Information please contact our EU representative GPSR@taylorandfrancis.com
Taylor & Francis Verlag GmbH, Kaufingerstraße 24, 80331 München, Germany

www.ingramcontent.com/pod-product-compliance
Lightning Source LLC
Chambersburg PA
CBHW070302230426
43664CB00014B/2612